YOUR BODY IS SPEAKING

CONNECT WITH YOUR BODY'S WISDOM TO LIVE
YOUR MOST EMPOWERED & ELEVATED LIFE

YOUR BODY IS SPEAKING

JEN AKS

herStories LLC
New York, NY

herStories LLC
New York, NY
Copyright © 2025 by Copyright Holder. All rights reserved.
Library Congress Control Number: 2025915586
Paperback ISBN: 979-8-9985158-1-1
eBook ISBN: 979-8-9985158-0-4
Hardcover ISBN: 979-8-9985158-2-8

Book cover design by theBookDesigners
Interior design by Damonza
Editorial production by KN Literary Arts

www.jenaks.com

To my mother,
who showed me what true strength and resilience look like,
who believed in me even when I couldn't believe in myself,
and who taught me to trust the wisdom of my
body long before I had words for it.

And to my children, my greatest teachers.
You remind me daily why this journey matters.
This book exists because you do.

CONTENTS

FOREWORD

Every once in a while, you meet people whose presence just captivates you. You get lost in their brilliance, and their energy just lights up your world.

Jen Aks is one of the people.

From the moment I met her, I was hooked. I immediately knew I was in the presence of someone who had embodied transformation. We dove into a conversation about **The Power of Gesture**® and started trading stories about our breakthroughs and insights. I was impressed with her ability to put words to something that feels so sacred... so spiritual... so indescribable. But, somehow, she spoke about emotion, healing, and the body with a clarity that felt like grace, and I knew then I was in the presence of a true master.

The first time I experienced freedom by listening to my body's intelligence came during a particularly heavy season in my life. Struggling with depression and uncertainty, I found solace in prayer, worship, and singing—practices I had always turned to in moments of difficulty. But one day, while I was alone at church, something unexpected happened.

While I was praying, listening to my music, and worshiping, I felt my body wanting to do something different—like a ballerina-type leap. Now, as a six-foot-five black dude and a former Division I athlete, I had never moved my body like that. In fact, I always felt insecure about moving my body in that way, outside of the typical "club" hand up and down movements. But at that moment, I followed my body's impulse.

And something incredible happened. As soon as I made that leap and allowed myself to move freely, the heaviness of the depression

I was facing started to shrink, then vanish. I felt so empowered, so free, that I just kept moving—for almost thirty minutes straight. I didn't want to leave that space. The freedom was so real and full that it felt like I was beneath an open portal and insights were "raining" down on me by the second.

I realized I had been ignoring my body for so long. As an elite athlete, everything I'd learned had taught me to mute my body—not listen to it. It didn't matter what my body was prompting me to do. Its job was to do as I said. Even after back surgery, I kept playing Division I football, shutting out the pain, ignoring the warning signs, and numbing my body with epidural shots and painkillers. I suppressed my body's voice, even when it was screaming for care and respect.

But that moment—dancing at my church—marked the beginning of a journey of recognizing, following, and listening to my body's impulses. It was the beginning of my learning to listen to my body's voice again. From there, I would discover intuitive eating and eventually dive fully into the practice of learning to follow my body's wisdom. Now, as a speaker and coach, my body has become a foundational key component of how I communicate, move audiences, and express myself. It is the conductor of the energy I share when I speak. It's the source of my power on stage, and following its nudges creates magic beyond my comprehension.

That's why this book is a must-read for anyone who knows, even deep down, that their ability to reach their full potential is directly connected to their ability to listen to their body.

Through story, style, science, her signature 3 E's framework, and **The Power of Gesture** practice, Jen offers readers a roadmap with practical tools to reclaim their power, heal from past wounds, and step into their most authentic, embodied life

This book isn't just a guide. It's an invitation to begin your own journey of reconnection.

And I truly believe that, just like I did, you will discover the strength, clarity, and freedom that only comes from within.

Enjoy the journey!

Darryll Stinson
2xTEDx Speaker | Story Architech | Executive Coach

A LETTER FOR YOU

Dear Reader,

Have you ever felt the pull to make a shift in your life, except something keeps getting in the way? That stirring inside—the one you can feel but can't quite understand yet you know something is off? From the outside, your life looks great. People depend on you, love you, and may even admire you. Yet deep down, something isn't right, as if there's a truth waiting to be heard.

For the longest time, I felt like I was living my life, being who I was supposed to be, following the path, but quietly disappearing inside of it. If you know that feeling—if you've felt this disconnect in your bones—I wrote this for you. This book was not written to give you more strategies or steps but instead to remind you that **the stirring inside is a call back to yourself**. It's awakening the kind of courage that lives quietly inside you, waiting to be heard. If you're even holding this book, it means something in you is already rising to meet that call. **You don't need to earn your way back to yourself— you just need to trust that you're already on the path.** You're not alone. I've been there, and I'm here now, walking right beside you.

For years, I didn't think I had the "right" words to express what I felt or needed, fearing I wouldn't do it in the "right" way. Yet, here I am, having written an entire book, wanting to share what I now know to be true: Your body has never stopped speaking to you. It's been whispering, nudging, trying to get your attention—not to overwhelm you, but to guide you. It's trying to remind you that you're still in there—and that you have the strength to return to your voice of truth, so it can guide you toward your highest, most empowered self.

We are wired to trust our instincts—a natural intelligence that's essential for survival. As hunters and gatherers, our ancestors relied on their bodies to sense danger, find food, and navigate their environment. They didn't overthink. They felt. They listened to the signals in their bodies. Whether it was a quickening heartbeat that warned of a predator. Tensed muscles signaling a readiness for action. An intuitive pull that may have caused a parent to protect a child from danger.

But somewhere along the way, we lost that connection. We started prioritizing logic over instinct, perfection over presence, and validation over truth. We learned to override our feelings, ignore the signs, and dismiss what we know to be real. Coming back to your body isn't just a return to something ancient and familiar; it's a necessary call to action when you're craving to live your truth.

Throughout this book, I'll guide you to listen, notice, and gently respond to what your body has been trying to tell you all along. Don't worry—I'll walk with you every step of the way. I have so many hopes for you as you read this book. But if I had to pick just one, it would be this: that you come to trust the stirrings within you—not as something to fear or suppress, but as signals from your body, telling you something important deserves your attention.

I believe that in order to live fully and freely, we must relearn what our ancestors knew so well: The body speaks to us. It warns. It guides. It protects and it knows our truth.

My question to you is—are you ready to listen?

INTRODUCTION

IT'S TIME TO LISTEN

IMAGINE A LIFE unburdened by the expectations of others. A life where you walk confidently, speak your truth without apology and trust that every choice you make is the right one. Imagine your true self—the one beneath fear or doubt—living fully expressed, out loud. Imagine a life when that inner voice whispers, "there's more," and you not only hear it, you act on it. This type of life is not only possible, it is waiting for you to grab hold of it.

It was my own journey back to my body that revealed something incredibly important—that disconnection from our **body wisdom** is a natural part of life and the return home is a necessary one. It's that cycle that is the human experience, and when we embrace it—not looking at it as a problem but instead as an opportunity—I believe that anything is possible.

When you stand firmly in your truth, your unique purpose awakens—benefiting not only yourself but rippling out to touch countless others.

Recognizing this pattern inspired me to create the 3 E's framework: **Embody. Empower. Elevate.** This is a roadmap that guides individuals home to themselves, just as it guided me. Throughout this book, we'll explore each phase deeply, where I will give you practical tools to awaken, listen to, and ultimately trust the voice from within.

This is not a quick fix or a cliché. It's a foundational framework for self-discovery and empowered growth. It helps you check in, notice where you are, develop the tools you need to listen with confidence, and most importantly, it brings you home to who you truly are, where the right guidance is waiting for you.

As a dance educator for over 30 years, I've seen the impact and influence that the body can have on our transformation. And yet, in so many healing and empowerment practices, the body is left behind because we spend so much time and focus on mindset. Practices like CBT, Growth Mindset, Reframing, and others have helped countless people shift limiting beliefs toward empowered thoughts. However, mindset alone is just part of the equation.

Mindset shifts how we think. Bodyset shifts how we feel. Just like mindset is a mental attitude, bodyset is a physical state. That's why I developed The Power of Gesture, a bodyset practice that bridges the connection between Mindset (your thoughts) and Bodyset (your emotions and sensations). When these align, they awaken your innate body wisdom—helping you get comfortable with your body, feel confident in yourself, and be able to communicate clearly what it is you want in your life. In the coming chapters, we'll explore what it means to bodyset with an approach grounded in science and real stories of transformation. You'll discover how this simple yet powerful practice creates a bridge between what you feel in your body and how you show up in your life, ultimately allowing you to make choices that are truly aligned with who you are.

Mindset shifts how we think. Bodyset shifts how we feel.

WHAT BECOMES POSSIBLE

The Power of Gesture reminds you that everything you need in order to make the right decisions for your life, exists within you. It will show you that intuitive nudges are whispering messages to be acknowledged rather than resisted, and that everyday moments—such as being silly when no one else is, crying at a movie when no one is shedding a tear, or having an opinion even when it's different from others'—are real, and more importantly, exactly right because they are all expressions of who you truly are.

Yet, society often discourages this kind of self-expression. From childhood, we're conditioned to color within the lines, to conform to expectations about our bodies, behaviors, and beliefs. These pressures from society, family, media, and generations past have taken us off track, where we give our power away. **What we need to remember is that outside pressures are exactly that: outside. They're expectations created by others to make sense of their world, not ours, not yours.**

The Power of Gesture is a gentle approach to help us get to know our emotions and appreciate where they came from. In this practice, we develop gratitude for hearing their stories and, as a result, understand ourselves through a lens of compassion, extending a hand toward each emotion as if we're saying, "I see you. Anger, what happened? I'm listening. Joy, what lifts you up? Tell me what you love to do."

This entire book and my mission is to empower you to be you—to break free from narratives that don't feel right so you can step boldly into alignment with your truth, and make decisions from that place. When we do this, something profound happens: our inner leader emerges. The one that has your back. The one that knows who you are, and what you want. Now, I invite you to pause here for a moment. Place one hand on your heart, one hand on your belly and close your eyes. Imagine a time when you felt clear, confident, most alive. Feel the presence of that strength. If you can't connect to a specific memory right now, that's perfectly fine. Create one in your mind - imagine yourself feeling strong, capable, unshakeable. Many times, your brain doesn't know the difference between a vivid image and a real memory. Use this as an approach for yourself to manifest this reality. That is your inner leader, your trusted guide. Allow this voice to rise, to expand and to show up for you now.

By the end of this book, you will have deepened your connection to courage, clarity, and confidence. You will be ready to speak without apology, take action despite fear, and to be heard even when it feels lonely. This is a journey home to you so that you can elevate and attract all that you are meant to.

HOW THE POWER OF GESTURE CAME ABOUT

Having spent my career studying, performing teaching the transformative power of movement, I thought I had mastered all that it could offer. Yet when the 2020 pandemic struck, it revealed its power in a way that I could never have predicted.

As the world confined itself to homes—isolated and desperate for connection—I saw humanity's need to heal its pain and celebrate its resilience. With doors closed, faces covered, and profound isolation settling in, it felt as though our humanity was being stripped away, altering each one of us.

The pandemic asked us to reflect on our past and consider our future. We had the opportunity to re-evaluate our identity, make decisions about the relationships we wanted to hold on to, and decide which ones we needed to let go of. This was a moment to look closely at ourselves, heal what had been neglected, and pave a new path forward. I knew that in order to make these choices, we had to become embodied first so that we could realign with our truth.

Despite the unknown and the fear, I began to walk a path that felt more natural than anything I had ever experienced in my life. I surrendered to not knowing where I was headed and chose to follow the guidance from within.

I started by reaching out to women I knew and asked if they would place their trust in what I was being led to do. I told them not to expect a roadmap, rather an exploration to what I felt would be extremely healing and empowering. As we sat together in Zoom rooms confined to a square, I invited them to share their feelings by asking questions about their experiences—what was helping them get through and how they were finding moments of release.

Being confined to virtual spaces, I had to get creative. I wanted the people I was working with to move the emotional energy in their bodies, yet knew the movement needed to stay close to the camera so I could see their eyes and feel their energy. I invited them to embody and express their emotions with their hands. What started as a simple request became one of the most profound discoveries of my life—that **these hand gestures had the ability to transform one's emotional state, provide insight, and empower self trust that provided comfort in a time where we needed it most.**

The hands became a bridge crossing our mental, spiritual and physical being, allowing the intangible to become tangible. Who knew we could hold our emotions, give them an identity, and get to know them so intimately with hand movement? Who knew we could rewire emotions connected to memories that once held us back and now could take us forward?

Without realizing it, I was developing what is now known as The Power of Gesture, a somatic experience that unlocks and empowers our kinesthetic and emotional intelligence, creating a path for transformation, hope, and celebration. This practice was 100 percent intuitive. There was no playbook, guide, or lesson plan. I made a choice to trust the guidance from within. And wow, am I glad I did!

Because we used just our hands, the practice became accessible for almost anyone, allowing me to work with hundreds of people from incredibly diverse backgrounds. People with physical disabilities could participate fully, as could those who'd never considered themselves "movement people" before. What began as a necessity born from a time that felt restricting, evolved into something far more profound— a universal language of embodiment available to everyone.

The Power of Gesture came from a place deep within me that I felt first and thought about second. I trusted that my body knew what to do, and this instinctive knowing has since been validated both by research in embodied cognition and by the hundreds of transformations I've witnessed in those who practice it.

WHAT IS THE POWER OF GESTURE?

The Power of Gesture is built on a foundation of three key components:

1. My 30-plus years as a dance educator, teaching children and adults how to use their bodies to learn, process, heal, and transform.
2. Research in embodiment and somatics.
3. Research on kinesthetic and emotional intelligence.

Let's dive into each of these a little deeper.

Embodiment and Somatic are both words we hear a lot, especially lately, so I want to take a moment to briefly explain them and their roles in The Power of Gesture.

Embodiment refers to the integration of mind and body, where we get into alignment with our emotions, sensations, and values. If you have ever played or are familiar with the game Jenga, you can visualize the stacking of blocks that create a tower. And if you don't know the game, just imagine building blocks one on top of the other. Now, imagine those blocks are your values, emotions, and sensations all in alignment which allows you to feel truthful, powerful, clear, and calm—as opposed to being out of alignment when our emotions feel out of control, scattered like when the Jenga blocks fall all over the floor.

Somatic comes from the Greek word *soma,* meaning *body,* and it refers to anything related to the body. Somatic approaches are often used in therapy to help people process emotions and trauma by deepening self-awareness. While somatic practices build awareness of the body, embodiment is about living that awareness.

Therapists like Bessel van der Kolk, Alice Miller, and Peter Levine have shifted our understanding of the mind-body connection and are experts in helping us recognize how trauma, emotions, and life experiences are stored in the body. They have given us the language and tools to recognize that the body remembers, and more importantly, that it knows how to help us process, understand, and heal.

Peter Levine says, "The sensations and feelings that are imprinted within our bodies contain the secrets to transformation." This emphasizes the importance of listening to our internal cues. Alice Miller says, "Our bodies have a sense of truth that is independent of what we consciously believe." This reinforces the need to remain curious and know there is so much wisdom within us. Bessel van der Kolk teaches us, "We have to be able to feel safe in our own bodies in order to begin to trust our surroundings and the people around us." This truth lights up everything I believe about our journey toward powerful connection. Think about it—how can we possibly create meaningful relationships with ourselves

Who knew we could hold our emotions, give them an identity, and get to know them so intimately with hand movement?

7

and with others if we don't have trust within ourselves first? This is exactly why the work we're doing together matters so much. When we commit to truly knowing ourselves—our bodies, our emotions, our needs—we're not just doing personal development work. We're creating the foundation for the life we're meant to live and the relationships we're meant to have.

The more we embody, the more we are able to tap into two kinds of intelligence you may not even be aware you have: Kinesthetic and Emotional Intelligence. Kinesthetic Intelligence (KI) is your physical body's ability to be a tool for learning and communicating. Emotional Intelligence (EI) is the ability to recognize, understand, and manage your emotions and the emotions of others. Understanding the roles that kinesthetic and emotional intelligence play in our success is an absolute life shifter! I go into much more detail about these forms of intelligence later in the book.

Think about how you expressed yourself as a baby and toddler—with your hands and body, through gestures, right? You communicated your sadness, frustration, anger, joy, and love, all without words. Your parents knew when you were tired, hungry, or when you found something funny. They got to know you through your actions, not your words.

This connection remains powerful throughout our lives. When you move your hands intentionally—whether through gesture, writing, or creating art—you're activating a deep connection between your body and mind. The Power of Gesture taps into this innate relationship, using hand movements as a bridge between your thoughts and emotions. Each gesture becomes a tool to align your mind and body, helping you access deeper wisdom, communicate more authentically, and feel empowered in your daily life.

Later in this book, I'll share the fascinating science behind why this practice works so powerfully. But for now, know that The Power of Gesture is rooted in something you've always known how to do—it's wired into your nervous system from birth, you may have just forgotten how to access it. I believe that's why this practice creates such profound shifts so quickly. It's not about learning something new—it's about remembering a language your body has always spoken. A language that was there long before words. It's this innate wisdom which brings us back to the profound truth that so much of what you need is already within you, at your fingertips—the answers to your questions, the healing for your past, and the empowerment of your present and future self.

Wherever you are on your journey of life, the fact that you've picked up this book shows that you're ready to take a step toward elevating it. Congratulations on saying yes to yourself! By diving into this work, you're opening the door to a powerful modality that will help you reconnect with one of your greatest resources: your body. Together, we'll rediscover the most trusted guide—your internal system, designed to support, empower, and elevate you.

HOW IT WORKS AND WHEN TO USE IT

The Power of Gesture is simple—yet incredibly impactful. Whenever you feel overwhelmed, stuck, or simply want to connect more deeply with yourself, your hands become the bridge between what you feel inside and how you process it. You can use this practice anywhere—during a challenging meeting, in your car before walking into your home, or while sitting quietly in meditation.

Speaking of meditation, I would like to highlight something for you because it was a discovery for me that absolutely changed my life. If you are someone who has a meditation practice—even if it is just a couple of minutes, you can add The Power of Gesture to it. If you are someone who finds mediation hard because sitting still just doesn't work for you, check this out.

While traditional meditation asks us to sit still and quiet our thoughts (which is valuable) I found myself craving something more—a practice that would allow me to physically engage with what I was feeling, not just observe it. So, I brought my hands into the experience allowing them to become translators for my emotions. How cool! What I found was that I was able to bring abstract emotions—anxiety, grief, joy, confusion—and make them tangible. I was able to shape them, hold them, and transform them. Here's what happened. That flutter in my chest became an energy I could mold between my palms. That heaviness in my shoulders became a weight I could release through my fingertips. By using The Power of Gesture, the emotional energy is able to relax which allows our body to speak in a way where we can hear it. In essence, we're partnering with our emotions in a way that offers compassion and allows us to get our power back.

This isn't just intuition speaking—it's supported by research in embodied cognition showing how our physical movements directly influence our emotional processing. **When we gesture, we activate neural pathways that words alone cannot reach, creating new possibilities for healing and insight.**

Try this: Pause for a moment and close your eyes. Place your hands in front of you with palms facing up, and imagine a recent experience where you doubted yourself or felt anxious, worried, or stuck. Visualize that emotion and its energy sitting in your palms. Allow your mind and body to connect to this feeling. After holding it for a minute or so, say either aloud or quietly to yourself, "I see you, I've got you, I'm with you." You'd be surprised at how this small act of kindness toward yourself puts your body at ease and creates trust within. This is what Bessel van der Kolk refers to when he says, "We have to be able to feel safe in our own bodies in order to begin to trust our surroundings and the people around us." His message speaks to the importance of compassion and how necessary it is for making these internal shifts. When we embrace an emotion as if it's a child who needs to be heard and held, we transform the energy inside us, helping us feel better and trust ourselves more deeply.

By mastering The Power of Gesture, you will become more comfortable in listening to your body's wisdom, confident in who you are, and have the strength to stand up for how you feel because you will have created trust within yourself. **It is that trust in yourself that will allow you to pause, listen when your body speaks, and follow its lead—even when your mind hesitates.** You'll be able to face your fears, recognize when you're unhappy and have a tool to help you understand why. You will no longer need to rely on others; instead, you will rely on yourself. How empowering is that? You'll have the confidence to break free and walk your true path. You'll discover that you can peel away layers of fear and doubt, understanding that these may have been created by a world that measures value by a script that was not written by you. I am here to teach you how to shed this fundamental misunderstanding that society has led you to believe for far too long and guide you into a place of embodied and empowered living.

The language of the body is divine, period. There is no better teacher; and trust me, it is ready to guide you home—to your truth, to your passions, to all of the things you want to say and do in this lifetime. What may initially seem like a lonely path will ultimately become your greatest reward.

How does your life change knowing that:

- Your body tells you when you need something.
- Your body tells you when you are sad.
- Your body tells you when you are inspired.
- Your body tells you when you are happy.
- Your body tells you when you are angry.

- Your body tells you when you are ready to make a change.
- Your body tells you when a relationship is right or wrong for you.
- Your body tells you when it's time to ask for that promotion.
- Your body tells you when to say yes and when to say no.

The more you embrace this truth, the more you will go from wanting to live your truth part of the time, to living your truth all of the time. There is no better feeling than standing in your strongest, most authentic self.

BODYSET: BEYOND MINDSET TO EMBODIED WISDOM

Bodyset is a term that I came up with to describe the intentional practice of checking in with your body's wisdom with the intention to access truth. Our truth before we make a decision, to deepen our understanding of our emotions and to gain clarity on decisions that we might be struggling with. Think of it like a mindset, but for your body—a bodyset. An opportunity to prepare, just as athletes do before a game, or a performer, as they head to the stage. When we bodyset, we not only prepare our emotional and physical selves, we inquire to find truthful guidance within us.

Together, mindset and bodyset form a cycle that integrates the mind's logic and the body's intuitive truth, which can awaken and enlighten your entire being.

I spent two decades living out of alignment, disembodied, and struggling with crippling self-doubt, all because I based my self-worth on society's definition of what it means to be smart. It wasn't until my late 20s, when I hit rock bottom, that I decided this would no longer be my reality. Once I took control, my entire world changed.

This is when I learned about the multiple forms of intelligence and realized I had been evaluating myself against one form my whole life and coming up short. Learning about my strengths in other forms of intelligence completely changed my life and awakened my purpose. I rediscovered the wisdom within and began healing from what was arguably some of the most challenging years of my life. It was that awakening—combined with the innate power I felt in my body as a dancer—that helped me heal, re-embody, and get back to who I was meant to be.

By the time you reach the final page of this book, you will have mastered The Power of Gesture, which will help you stay connected with the truth of who you are and keep you grounded with confidence in the choices you make. You will be standing taller, feeling braver, and knowing that your body has the answers you need.

Listening to our truth can be scary and confronting. It can also sometimes mean disappointing others because we are listening to ourselves instead of them. This is an unconventional path, and it can feel tough at first. I wrote this book for you to soothe those fears and empower you to embrace them—to know that your fears are here to teach you and that your truth has your best interest at heart. Learning The Power of Gesture is going to help you understand those fears in a way that feels safe, gentle.

Being raw is powerful and vulnerability heals.

In this book, I reveal parts of my life that are extremely vulnerable and possibly risky to put on the page. Writing this has been uncomfortable at times, but I have remained committed because my biggest priority is helping you see yourself inside my stories and know that you are not alone. I want you to see that being raw is powerful, and that vulnerability heals and helps others do the same. There are many reasons why you may have picked up this book. You might desire more from life, yet feel guilty because others perceive you as already having so much. You may want to learn a new practice that will help you process your emotions on a regular basis. You may want to find a way to feel stronger, bolder and more confident in the decisions you make. Whatever your reason for reading and experiencing this book, here is what I ask of you:

1. Trust that whatever shows up is exactly right.
2. Be kind to yourself.
3. Be patient.
4. Allow your perspective to shift.
5. Embrace each emotion as a teacher.
6. Be proud of your courage to try something new.

This book is broken down into three parts: Embody. Empower. Elevate. **The 3 E's framework** serves as a guide for living because it provides comfort when you need it, validates where you are with research and practical tools, and remains simple to understand. In each section, I define the phase, explain why it matters, and show you how to apply it to transform your daily life.

HOW TO USE THIS BOOK

At the end of each chapter, you'll find Power of Gesture bodyset practice tailored to a theme that we just explored. It will be written out, and you'll have access to a QR code linking to a video where I will guide you through the exercise. I highly encourage you to read through the written version to familiarize yourself with the flow. Then, when you're ready to dive in, scan the QR code to experience the guided practice with me. I cannot wait! Over time, you will become comfortable with The Power of Gesture and may not need or want to read the exercise first; instead, going right to the video. With that said, the written version will always be there as a reference for your personal practice.

Every time you engage with The Power of Gesture, you're creating what I call a "moving mantra" with your hands. These mantras/gestures expand into a vocabulary of your own understanding and are deeply personal because they come from you, which makes them easier to remember and more meaningful. The best part? Because you are only using your hands, you can use these moving mantras anytime, anywhere. Feeling stressed at a dinner with friends, coworkers, or family? Excuse yourself for a moment, step into the bathroom, and bodyset with your moving mantra. In just a few moments, you will be able to shift from feeling overwhelmed to powerful, anxious to calm, centered, and ready to engage from a grounded place.

I invite you to grab a journal, a pad of paper, or your computer to keep track of your experiences along the way. When I prompt you with questions, write the chapter along with your answer so you can easily come back to it later.

You will also see affirmations throughout the book. When you see one, I invite you to read it, put the book down, get into The Power of Gesture bodyset position, which I describe below. After a few breaths, repeat the affirmation three times slowly. By combining the bodyset position along with saying the affirmations, you will be expressing a gesture of love, connection, strength and support for yourself. This is a quick way to reset your emotional energy efficiently.

Let's get started with a pledge.

A BODYSET PRACTICE: A PLEDGE TO YOURSELF

Each time we begin The Power of Gesture exercise, we will start with the official bodyset position—one hand on your heart, one hand on your belly, and most of the time, you will close your eyes. With this particular pledge exercise, you will keep your eyes open, and while your hands are on your body, read the pledge slowly. The important thing here is to notice how your body is feeling while saying these words.

I, [Name], make this sacred promise to myself:

- To honor my needs, my truth, and my inner wisdom without judgment.
- To recognize that putting myself first is not selfish but instead a divine act of self love.
- To reconnect to who I am at my core, standing firmly for what I believe with compassion and courage.
- To embrace this commitment as a gift to myself, knowing that by allowing the leader within to have a strong voice, my children, my colleagues, and all those I love will benefit.
- To trust that leading from within is the key to unlocking my highest potential.
- To face my fears with love, curiosity and compassion.

How did reading that pledge make you feel? If you feel called to it, take a moment to journal about your experience. Do you feel a sense of relief, empowerment, or a spark of excitement? Are you nervous? Curious? Afraid? Just so you know, I get it all! And here is my invitation to you: Let these feelings serve as signals and insights, guiding toward rediscovering and remembering who you truly are and all that you're capable of. I'll keep emphasizing this because my purpose is to guide you toward your highest truth and help you reconnect with your strength.

> **Empowered Affirmation**: *I am ready to listen, to grow, and to lead from within—starting now.*

PART ONE
EMBODY

WHAT IS IT?

BECOMING EMBODIED IS about awareness and reconnection—tuning into yourself, getting comfortable with listening to your body's wisdom and realigning with what truly matters to you. It's a shift from living according to external expectations to living from an internal knowing, where your inner truth leads the way instead of outside influences dictating your path. Remember the reference earlier to the Jenga game? I'm going to bring it back because it's a great way to visualize the concept of what it means to become embodied.

Imagine those blocks stacked one on top of the other, representing what matters most to you—your values, truths, and identity. When the blocks are carefully aligned, they create a solid foundation and core strength, allowing you to feel balanced, focused, and strong enough to make decisions from that place.

Now, imagine the structure that you created gets wobbly, starts to fall apart, and comes crashing down. That image represents you feeling off balance, shaky, or completely out of control. This is when we become disembodied, getting out of alignment where we start doubting ourselves, question our choices and feel unsafe inside of ourselves.

WHY DOES IT MATTER?

Becoming embodied matters because it creates a foundation of strength where confidence can soar, clarity has the opportunity to be consistent, and happiness is felt. If we skip the work of becoming embodied, here's what happens. We stay in jobs or relationships that drain us because we are unclear about what we want and not strong enough to make the necessary changes we need to. We lose ourselves in other people's opinions, expectations, judgments and become easily swayed by what others think instead of standing firmly in our truth. By not becoming embodied, we're constantly in reaction mode, letting life happen to us rather than taking charge and leading it from a place that feels right.

While becoming embodied can feel challenging, it's also quite beautiful because it's the process of reconnecting and rediscovering who we truly are. It's an intimate "getting to know yourself" phase that creates comfort with in our body and deepens inner trust. It's this trust that becomes your foundation, which allows you to make confident decisions and face life's challenges with certainty. That's huge!

HOW WILL IT IMPROVE YOUR LIFE?

When we are embodied, so much opens up for us. First and most importantly, we have an awareness about ourselves that is incredibly empowering. We have spent the time to get to know how we feel, why we feel it, and understand how to make shifts when we need to. Can you imagine talking to your spouse, partner, boss, friend or child when they are triggering you left and right and instead of burning up inside—wanting to yell and fight back or defend yourself—you have the skills to stay in control and calm? I mean, who wouldn't want that? That alone can save your life because you will have avoided all the stress and replaced it with ease. We know how much stress contributes to illness, so having a way to combat that is a big deal.

As an embodied person, you know how to pause and "feel" into decisions. You now have a tool to re-center and call the shots. You have more clarity on your path because you understand yourself so well that you know what choices are right for you. Honestly, I could spend the rest of this book explaining the benefits of why this work is important, but I would like to get started with a simple exercise.

Here are a few questions to assess your current relationship with your body's wisdom. These will help you discover where you stand now, so you can measure how far you travel as we move forward together. Read one question at a time. After reading the questions, close your eyes, pause, and notice the answer and the sensation or feeling that shows up. Let go of any need to analyze or understand, instead, just notice.

1. Do you know what it means to listen to your body?
2. Do you rely on your body's wisdom to guide you during tough moments or decisions?
3. How often do you dismiss your feelings, believing they aren't relevant?

Wherever you are right now—whether you're unsure how to listen to your body, wish you could rely on it more, or already feel in tune and want to strengthen that even more, you will expand into a greater awareness, comfort and confidence.

One of my favorite quotes by Stephen Covey is, "Begin with the end in mind." This simple wisdom has always inspired me to envision the destination—to see the end goal clearly—so I can get excited about the journey and start taking the steps to get there.

With that said, here is an important truth: before we can fully reclaim this embodied state, it will be helpful to understand how we lost it in the first place. Our journey toward becoming embodied asks us to acknowledge the disconnection first. Like a map that marks both the starting point and destination, we need to know where we are to chart our course forward. This is not about reliving experiences or blaming others; this is about deepening self-awareness so that we can move forward with an understanding about who we are, why we feel the way we feel, what we want, and where we want to go. Together, with intention and love, we will navigate this journey and arrive bolder, stronger, more alive, and courageous than ever before. Here we go!

CHAPTER 1

DISEMBODIED LIVING: MAPPING YOUR JOURNEY AWAY FROM SELF

By owning your disconnection story and approaching it with curiosity, you unlock what you need in order to grow into the person you are meant to be.

WE COME INTO this world with our eyes wide open, innocent, and free. There seem to be no barriers or limitations in front of us, just a freedom in our souls that allows for unapologetic expression. It's an inherent connection to our bodies and emotions—a natural state of embodiment. As babies, we cry, laugh out loud, and ask for what we want and when we want it. We are free from judgment, compromise, and the burdens of worry and doubt. Yet, as we grow older, we start to experience those things that threaten the pure joy of who we truly are. For some of us it's an educational system focused on standardized testing, for others it happens gradually through societal pressures, or family dynamics that—even with the best intentions—may not create space for authentic expression. The path toward disconnection is different for all of us, yet no matter what, it has the power to overshadow our truths and dim our light, getting lost in beliefs that we didn't have a say in.

A thought pattern that takes so many of us out of alignment is the common "I should" statements. I should be able to be as successful as him/her. I should have won that game. I should have scored higher on that test. I should have stayed in that relationship longer and given it more time. I should be able to lose weight like my friend because she did it so easily. I should have had more than one child, so my one child didn't have to be alone. I should know how to stand up for myself. I should. I should. I should. Says who? These statements take us way out of our alignment and create a disconnection from our unique gifts. Here's the thing. You SHOULD be exactly where you are. You should feel what you feel, always! How do I know that? Because you are feeling it. The truth is, you *should* have been in that relationship for the length of time that it lasted because it took that long to learn what you needed to know. You *should* have changed your major in college because you realized that the first one wasn't right for you. You *should* have had five different career paths because each has led you to where you are now.

I am open to understanding my past and trust in my power to create a future aligned with my truth.

I am right here, alongside you, comforting your past and empowering your present. I know what it feels like to hold that secret of doubt, that weight that keeps you playing small. What I want for you now is to transform that doubt into your superpower. By owning your part in your disconnection story and approaching it with curiosity, you can unlock what you need to grow into the person you want to be. I will share mine with you now.

FACING THE LIMITING STORIES WE TELL OURSELVES

When I was growing up, there was a strong emphasis on standardized tests and grades as the primary measure of intelligence. Because I didn't do great on either, I created a story about myself that I wasn't smart.

My struggles went beyond the tests; traditional teaching methods in the classroom didn't resonate with me either. It felt like the teachers were talking *at* me rather than *to* me. Textbooks were the primary tool for learning, and they lacked the type of engagement I craved. I knew I needed to interact with the material differently, but I had no idea what that looked like and felt ashamed that I couldn't figure it out. **I didn't realize back then that the teaching approach focused solely on the left brain, emphasizing logical intelligence, while leaving the right brain, where our creativity and emotional connections take place, out of the learning process.** This rigid, one-size-fits-all approach to education left me feeling overlooked, misunderstood, boxed in, unseen, and alone—not just by others but also by myself. The more I tried to think my way through my insecurities, the more misaligned and disembodied I felt. It was as if there was a tear splitting me in half, and no matter how hard I tried, I couldn't sew it back together.

My struggle was intensified within the walls of my own home because my brother effortlessly excelled academically. The family looked at him as an intellectual prodigy. Of course, his success deserved to be acknowledged and celebrated, yet each time my mother referred to him as "my star," my body felt sad. I remember feeling my heart ache because I was jealous, wishing that was me. I wanted nothing more than to excel in school, yet I felt stuck in this cloud of doubt because I wasn't able to connect in a way that resonated. The weight became a burden I carried for years.

Do you remember Trivial Pursuit? It was a popular game that always showed up at parties in high school and college. This was a game that required knowledge about history and the world in a way that just felt over my head. As silly as this may sound, you cannot imagine what this game did to my body. Whenever it hit the table, my heart would race, my head would burn up, and my stomach would flip. Just the appearance of the game created the most intense sensations of not belonging and a deep sense of unworthiness. It felt like I was on a wild roller coaster ride, trying desperately to calm everything down inside of my body—all because I was scared I wouldn't know the answers and would look stupid in comparison to everyone else. I would always find a way out. I couldn't breathe, so I would excuse myself and go to the bathroom to throw up or head outside for fresh air.

In my twenties, I had two significant relationships, both with men who graduated with top honors from Ivy League schools. In both relationships, I would question, "Why me?" I found it ironic and comical that I attracted such "smart" guys and yet somehow fit in perfectly with their friends and families. It caused me to wonder if maybe, just maybe, I wasn't inadequate at all and perhaps there was more to intelligence than test scores. Unfortunately, those whispers of doubting remained whispers, not nearly loud enough to combat all the years of built-up insecurity. Even though there was a lingering of another perspective, I continued to feel trapped under a heavy load of limiting beliefs, suffocating and unable to break free. It wasn't until the invitation—that I will tell you about in the next section—that I realized just how bad it was.

WHAT JFK JR., SELF-DOUBT, AND ROCK BOTTOM CAN TEACH US ALL

My heart stopped, and my breath got caught in my throat. I felt immobilized and numb. At 27 years old, I received an invitation to go to dinner with a major celebrity, John F. Kennedy Jr., and his wife, Carolyn Bessette-Kennedy. By the way, this was not an invitation for several people or a party where we would say a casual hello. This was an invitation for an intimate dinner with the two of them and two of us—me and my, "ivy league" boyfriend at the time. I was overwhelmed with anxiety, not because this was the son of a former president but because this proposal put me eye to eye with my darkest demons of self-criticism and doubt.

My boyfriend casually mentions that we're having dinner with JFK Jr. For him, it was no big deal because they had grown up together and were good friends. However, for me, this invitation landed very differently. The moment he told me, my heart started pounding, and my entire body went numb. Hearing JFK Jr.'s name instantly created images of textbooks and history lessons in my head. I pictured myself at the dinner table, talking about world politics, healthcare, social issues, and classic books. You would have thought I was invited to a policy briefing in the West Wing instead of a friendly dinner. I felt sure I'd be put on trial, berated with questions about books I hadn't read, grades I hadn't earned, and questions I couldn't answer. Crazy right? Well, you could definitely say that I was dis-embodied and completely out of alignment. I had created a drama in my head where I was the main character standing there ashamed, seeing all fingers pointing at me, saying, "You're not smart enough." "You're not worthy." "You have nothing to contribute to a conversation with someone like JFK Jr. What are you even doing here?" The angst flooding my body was like a tornado I couldn't escape. I had no sense of reality. Lost in a nightmare of my own making, I ended up declining this once-in-a-lifetime invitation.

I did what I always did in moments of complete self-doubt and disassociation: I retreated to my safe place, the shower, where I found comfort from the warm water falling on my body. Feeling ashamed, I slithered to the floor, curled up in a ball, and cried. I was not only naked physically; I was naked emotionally. I held my pounding heart and aching stomach, desperately searching for answers. I was deeply disappointed that I had allowed this insecurity to hijack my life so aggressively. I had been used to versions of this throughout my life, but this was the worst. I sat there feeling the smallest I had ever felt and ashamed like never before. This was my rock bottom. I had given up on myself and wasn't sure how I would recover.

When we ignore our body's signals, it's like telling ourselves, "What you have to say doesn't matter." The American Psychological Association says that "ignoring our body's signals can have significant consequences on our mental and physical well-being. Research indicates that neglecting these internal cues may increase the risk of mental health disorders, including eating disorders and suicidal behavior." Years later, having almost three decades of experience and after doing substantial research, I now know that by choosing to face our truths, even when they play a role in our struggles, we are not only taking brave steps but critical ones toward living and leading a life of fulfillment, authenticity and success.

When we lean into our body anxiety with curiosity rather than judgment, we activate the part of our brain responsible for emotional regulation. Research shows that naming and acknowledging emotions can calm the amygdala, which is the brain's alarm system, and shift us from a reactive state to a more regulated one. The Power of Gesture is a tool to help us do that. When we bodyset, we are able to deactivate the fight-or-flight response and engage the parasympathetic nervous system, which promotes relaxation and calm. Can you imagine having learned how to do this when we were young? We would be better equipped to handle moments of doubt, stress, and anxiety in our lives and build our resilience to deal with discomfort, doubt, insecurity, or shame. Unfortunately, that's not the case, and it was certainly not for me. As I sat on the shower floor, curled up in a ball, I didn't have a bodyset tool. However, something else pretty extraordinary happened that would change the course of my life.

As hard as the moment was, my body's reaction was the exact information I needed to make one of the most important decisions of my life. After sitting there for a while, disappointed, frustrated and deeply sad with myself, a presence came over me, and I heard: "How long? How long are you going to stay stuck in this limiting belief that has had you disempowered for so many years?" I knew deep down that I was more than this. I knew that I had allowed society to define me before I could define myself. Underneath what felt like an impossible belief and story to rise above, I had this overwhelming feeling that there was so much to learn and so much more I was meant to become. **There were no easy guides, no ready answers, and no scripted path to follow, yet I felt an undeniable calling, a presence deep within, urging me to stand up and take action.** It was time to take control and allow this moment to become my teacher—the catalyst to find out who I was, how I learned, and what I was capable of.

This was the moment that I made the decision to break free from the limiting beliefs that had dominated my life for two decades. I embraced the discomfort, got out of my head, into my body, chose to get curious, and listen so that I could remember who I was. I didn't know how I would do it, but I knew I had to begin the journey home to me.

After I surrendered, I felt an overwhelming sense of calm. It was almost as if I was giving myself the biggest and most divine hug of my life. Did I have a specific embodiment tool? Did I know what I was doing? No. So instead, I followed my instinct, my gut—my body. For years, my shame, pain, and doubt were internally screaming, showing up loud, and in turmoil, causing massive chaos in my body. After surrendering, I felt my nervous system calm down, and I realized something so profound: These emotions weren't going to hurt me. They were simply crying out for attention. I found myself feeling empathetic toward them, looking to understand how they evolved. **I decided to honor these parts by leaning into their stories to understand their pain. It was as if there were several little people inside of my soul with emotions attached to experiences that needed to be processed and healed.** It was my job to make room for their voices, to scoot over and pull up more seats at the table.

Think about a moment when you felt overwhelmed, when you were flooded with emotions like anger, sadness, fear, or confusion. Now, instead of trying to push these feelings away, judging, or labeling them, try to imagine them as little people inside you, each one holding a story that hasn't yet been heard. What might they be trying to tell you? Picture these emotions waiting patiently (or not-so-patiently) for you to acknowledge them. How do they show up? Where do you feel them most?

PROMPTS FOR YOUR YOUNGER SELF:

- Do you remember when self-doubt or disconnection from your truth started to show up in your life?
- Can you name a specific experience(s)?
- What message would have helped you feel seen and valued in that moment?

PROMPTS FOR YOUR ADULT SELF:

- Do you silence your voice at social gatherings because you feel your words won't come out right?
- Have you ever had an idea that you wanted to explore but held back because you thought people would not take it seriously?
- Have you ever ignored a gut feeling about a person or situation because you couldn't logically explain why something felt off?

Take a moment to notice how you feel right now and send some love to whatever emotion(s) are showing up. Remember, these are just "parts" of you, not the whole of who you are. Later in the book, we'll dive deeper into understanding these parts and explore tools to work with them. For now, I hope that reframing how we engage with emotions can offer you a sense of relief—knowing that these parts are messengers to honor because they are here to teach us, not hurt us. Now, let's turn our attention to how the expectations in your life might have contributed to your disembodiment story even more. Understanding this can open the door to seeing how the voices of others—parents, teachers, peers—have quietly shaped how we show up in our body, giving us some clarity to start untangling what's truly ours from what we've absorbed along the way.

WHAT DID "THEY" EXPECT OF YOU?

As children, with so many expectations and personalities influencing how and what we should feel, it's no wonder we become doubtful and disconnected. As a result, many times, we tend to make decisions from our minds alone, which cuts out so much of where truth resides. It's almost as if we turn our back on our best friend, abandoning the very thing we can count on the most: our body. The good news is that we are able to realign, reconnect and invite that source back into its role—to be our guiding light, the one that we can really count on.

With your digital or written journal, start to recall the expectations that were placed on you while growing up. You can list the "rules" given to you from these common sources:

- Parents or caregivers
- Siblings, especially older ones
- Teachers
- Friends or a peer group
- Church, clergyperson, or a religious group

As you remember the "rules" you grew up with, write them down. Bodyset by placing one hand on your heart, one hand on your belly, and close your eyes. Ask yourself these two questions:

1. How did this rule or expectation make me feel?
2. Where do I feel it in my body?

Notice what shows up and take a moment to journal about it. Remember, this moment is about deepening self awareness—charting your map forward by understanding the roots of disconnection.

We are almost at the point where we take this awareness and begin to reconnect, re-embody, remember, and realign with the power that rests within us. Before we move forward, let's take a moment to consider another factor that might have contributed to your sense of disconnection: the impact of labels, insults, and social conditioning you may have absorbed along the way. Let's dive in a bit here and then follow up by experiencing The Power of Gesture for the first time. I cannot wait!

LABELS, INSULTS, AND SOCIAL CONDITIONING

The words of others can have an enormous impact on our bodies, taking us out of alignment. They have a way of making an imprint that can sometimes last decades, especially when we are young and don't know how to process the label or understand it. Often, we feel the sting of words even when they're disguised in backhanded compliments or humor. I have always disliked when people use humor as an excuse by saying, "Lighten up. It was meant to be funny." And then it gets worse because they turn it on you by saying, "Why are you taking this so seriously?" My question is, in what world is calling someone "fat," "too skinny," "sloppy," "flaky", "lazy", "weird", "bossy", or "too sensitive" funny? Yet, for whatever reason, there are people in the world who either don't care or have no sense of how damaging these "labels" can be and what impact they may have on someone's life.

These small comments have a way of sticking to us like glue and making us feel less-than and insignificant. Research supports how body-shaming and labeling can have a severe impact on the mental health of others. For example, Puhl and Heuer (2010) highlight that weight-based teasing and labeling contribute to significant emotional distress, including anxiety, depression, and body dissatisfaction. Rodgers et al. (2015) emphasizes that even "seemingly" minor negative comments about appearance can act as triggers for body image and eating disorders. Labels are not harmless; they stick with us, shape self-perception, and can absolutely add to our disconnection story.

Words matter and making a small shift can make a huge difference. For example, if a parent is trying to discipline their child by saying, "You are lazy," instead, they could say, "You are being lazy right now." Simply adding the "right now" lands in our body differently and can shift the course of how that person sees themselves. Adding "right now" means right now, it doesn't mean always. When you leave it at "You're lazy," it can be interpreted as *I am a lazy person* when, in fact, the person is only being lazy right now, at that moment. Do you see the difference? There is a process in the brain called the Reticular Activating System (RAS) which is like a filter, sifting through the messaging and highlighting what aligns with our beliefs about ourselves. So, for example, if we focus on a label that we are lazy, RAS will reinforce this belief, magnify it, and confirm it. Then, it will reinforce the story that we believe to be true by repeating it over and over again. This thought pattern creates an energy associated with the belief that stays in the body and creates memories with these feelings, which further adds to our disconnection.

With all of that said, we have the power to peel away the disempowering thoughts and replace them with ones that uplift and empower us. Joseph Nguyen, author of *Don't Believe Everything You Think*, says, "We just need to let go of listening to our mind and go beyond it by tuning into something greater that will not only help you survive but to thrive." I think back to elementary school, when I was told that the beauty mark on my face was a mole that would grow hair and become "witch-like and evil." I remember the sting of embarrassment and the insecurity that followed. I tried to do anything I could to hide this mole. It was hard to do because it was in the center of my face. After years of being made fun of, something

That knot in your stomach, that flutter in your chest—these aren't random sensations. They're messengers guiding you home.

shifted in me. By middle school, I decided to look at my mole as a beauty mark. I chose to view it as the thing that made me unique. I was young and didn't realize what I was doing until much later. I shifted my perspective and took control of the narrative. Looking back now, I realize how powerful that was.

LET'S SUMMARIZE WHAT WE KNOW

1. **Disconnection Is a Journey, Not a Destination:** We weren't born disconnected from our bodies. This separation happened gradually through expectations, labels, and external pressures that taught us to doubt our innate wisdom. This separation happened through experiences that taught us to question ourselves. Here's the great news! If we learn to disconnect, we can absolutely learn to reconnect.

2. **"Shoulds" Can Steal Our Power:** Every time you tell yourself "I should be different," consider that you're abandoning yourself. When you catch yourself in a "should" spiral, pause and ask: "Says who?" That will interrupt the habit and help you realign with a healthy perspective.

3. **Your Body Speaks Wisdom:** That knot in your stomach, that flutter in your chest—these aren't random sensations. They're messengers guiding you home.

Peeling Off the Labels & Reclaiming Your Truth

We've explored a bit about our disconnection story and the labels that may have contributed to it. Now, I'm going to take you through The Power of Gesture: Peeling Off the Labels & Reclaiming Your Truth. I'm going to modify it here in the book; however, you can experience a longer version by scanning the QR code at the end of this chapter or by visiting www.jenaks.com/yourbodyisspeaking, where you will find The Power of Gesture chapter videos. Press play, and I will be there to guide you through experience. I can't wait!

The Power of Gesture invites us to embody our dark and light. What holds us back and what moves us forward. I believe that in order to elevate our lives, we must become curious about all of who we are, not just part of who we are. To look at ourselves honestly and move forward from that place. This keeps us in authentic alignment, which then helps us create the life we desire and deserve. Let's begin.

STEP 1: INTENTION

Find a comfortable position and take a moment to **bodyset**. Close your eyes, place one hand on your heart, and one hand on your belly. Take a few deep breaths and state the following intention either quietly in your mind or out loud: "I am ready to release labels and limiting beliefs that no longer serve me, embracing my true self with confidence and compassion."

STEP 2: IDENTIFY

While keeping your eyes closed for another moment, reflect on a label that you have carried in your life and feel has contributed to your disconnection story. Allow your mind to take you to a memory where you heard the label, experienced it in some way, and felt it.

Here are some examples:

- "I'm too much."
- "I'm too emotional."
- "I'm bad at relationships."

1. Name your label.
2. Name how it makes you feel.
3. Notice where you feel it in your body.

STEP 3: GESTURE #1: EMBODY

This is where things get creative, and by getting creative with our heavier emotions, that alone helps us shift. The information you identified—the label, how it makes you feel, and where you feel it in your body—is what you need to create your first gesture. There is no right way to do this; however, I will offer this: Typically, an emotion that feels limiting most often creates a gesture that contracts. For example, your hands may clench by making fists, or your upper body may cave inward. Your chin may move down toward your chest, or your hands may rest over your eyes.

STEP 4: IDENTIFY

Now imagine yourself feeling the opposite, free of the label, where you feel empowered by overcoming this limiting belief. If you cannot connect to a memory, it's okay. You can create one. As I mentioned earlier, many times the mind doesn't know the difference. So use this as an opportunity to manifest this reality. I invite you to add an affirmation to deepen your connection.

Here are some examples:

- "I AM creative and unique in my own way."
- "I AM enough just as I am."
- "I honor my emotions and see them as a strength."

1. Name the new label.
2. Notice how it makes you feel.
3. Notice where you feel it in your body.

STEP 5: GESTURE #2: EMBODY

Use the information above to create gesture #2. When feeling confident, gestures tend to be more expansive. Feel free to use that as inspiration to create yours.

Here are some examples:

- Stretching arms wide open to symbolize liberation.
- Placing hands over the heart to embrace self-love.
- Lifting hands up over the head, welcoming strength and encouragement.

STEP 6: INTEGRATE

Allow yourself to integrate both gestures by moving back and forth from the restriction to the expansion several times. This is where the transformation happens. By giving yourself the opportunity to experience the natural duality, you are allowing both parts to be heard. This is a practice of acceptance and curiosity that deepens self-awareness and invites an elevated state of being. This also creates ease in the body so we can see and feel clearly to make the right choices for our lives.

TIPS FOR GESTURE PRACTICE

- **Bodyset:** You know how sprinters start a race with their hands on the ground? The Power of Gesture has a "ready, set" position, too. Place one hand on your heart, one hand on your belly, and close your eyes. This is the official The Power of Gesture bodyset position. It's neutral. It gives you a moment to gather yourself before you embody your emotion.

- **Move slowly**: Our daily lives are fast-paced, so slowing down with this practice is intentional. It not only calms the nervous system, but it also gives you an opportunity to listen to what your body wants to say. Your emotions are dying to tell you how they feel, so let them.

- **Repeat:** Repetition is important because it gives the body more time to process the emotion. We are doing this to learn, understand, and transform what no longer serves us, so patience is necessary. Once you embody the supportive emotion (Gesture #2) that represents what you *do* want to be aligned with, you will find even more understanding and release. We will get to that, soon.

- **Music:** Choose a piece of music that inspires you. I like to play instrumental music because, otherwise, the lyrics may put a thought in my mind that I don't align with. Using instrumental music allows our story to be the lyrics. With that said, it's a personal choice, so do what feels best to you.

STEP 7: JOURNAL

I invite you to document how your body feels after the practice and reflect on any new realizations that may have been made. Writing about this process creates a record of your journey, helping you track your transformation and return to it later for inspiration.

> **Empowered Affirmation:** *I release the labels that no longer serve me and instead define myself on my own terms.*

Ready to dive deeper? This QR code will take you to The Power of Gesture: Peeling Off the Labels & Reclaiming Your Truth video, where you'll join me for a full immersive experience that brings these concepts to life.

Before we close this chapter, I want to offer this. Labels don't always have a negative effect. Depending on our level of awareness and emotional maturity, we can use labels to support and uplift those around us. In 2019, I was writing and directing a show for National Dance Institute. I was sitting at Starbucks with one of my mentors and great friends, and she made a comment that completely shifted my perspective of how I saw myself. I was struggling to express my vision for show I was creating and she turned to me and said, "Jen, you are an artist; whatever you create is going to be brilliant." I remember feeling stunned and shocked; she literally took my breath away. My reaction was not in response to her telling me that whatever I produced would be brilliant; it was that she noticed that I was an "artist." As someone who has spent my entire life in the arts community—performing, teaching, mentoring, and choreographing—I knew I was an artist, but it was not a label I thought people associated with me. It was amazing how a positive label impacted my life. I stood taller, felt stronger in my expression, and believed that what I had to say mattered. I remember feeling this surge of empowerment run throughout my entire body, which strengthened my perspective on how I saw myself. My confidence changed in an instant. Used in this way, a label can positively impact someone's life. So, I invite you to try it because when you make someone feel great, it inevitably lifts you up as well.

In the next chapter, we will explore what it means to reconnect to the full you! The you that came into this world with no inhibitions. The you that expressed freely, fiercely, and unapologetically. Get ready to go on a ride that may feel bumpy yet entirely worth it. Bumpy because the work we are exploring asks you to engage with your emotions, and that can feel scary. I want to remind you that The Power of Gesture is a gentle approach toward getting to know yourself. It will also help you reset in any given moment and assist you in handling yourself with care. Yes, it requires vulnerability and a willingness to let go, but here's the important thing to know.. Joy is on the other side of pain. Enlightenment is on the other side of feeling stuck. Self-worth is on the other side of shame. I am here for all of it—with you, beside you, and cheering you on! By the end of the next chapter, you will no longer look outside yourself for the answers. Yes, you will seek guidance here and there, but you will trust yourself enough to know that your choice is the right one.

CHAPTER 2

RECONNECTING TO THE BODY: RESTORING YOUR INNATE WISDOM

*Our bodies know how to stand strong and inform
us of what we need. Our job is to notice, listen, ask,
and surrender to the guidance from within.*

RECONNECTING TO THE body is an incredibly exciting concept because it's where you return home to the truest version of yourself. It's like a reunion, an invitation to rediscover the wisdom and power that's always been within you.

Before we dive in, I want to explore some of the words we touched on in the previous sections. Some may have been familiar, and others may not have been. They are words that I will be using frequently throughout the book and sit at the center of this work, so I want to take a moment to review them.

1. **Embody or Embodiment** refers to the integration of mind and body, where we get into alignment with our emotions, sensations, and values.

2. **Somatic** comes from the Greek word *soma*, meaning *body* and refers to anything related to the body.

3. **Kinesthetic Intelligence** is the ability to connect with and understand how your body is a tool for learning and communication.

4. **Emotional Intelligence** is the ability to recognize, understand, and manage your emotions and the emotions of others.

5. **Bodyset** is a physical state that aligns your body's sensations and emotions, complementing mindset to create comfort in the body, confidence within yourself, and the ability to effectively communicate what it is you want.

6. **The Power of Gesture** is an embodiment practice that aligns mindset (your thoughts) and bodyset (your emotions and sensations) to awaken and empower what is already within you: your body's wisdom.

THE SCIENCE BEHIND THE POWER OF GESTURE

While The Power of Gesture was born from my intuition, powerful science helps explain why this work creates such profound transformation. Recent neuroscience research reveals something amazing: our hands have a unique relationship with the brain, with more cortical tissue dedicated to controlling and sensing our hands than nearly any other part of the body.

"When physical gestures are performed intentionally," as my friend and board-certified neurologist Ryan Williamson, M.D. explains, "especially slowly and with emotion—they can stimulate the parasympathetic nervous system, which is the body's rest-and-digest mode. This has been well demonstrated in various practices, such as yoga and Tai Chi. Unlike intense or sudden movements, these calm, rhythmic gestures can signal safety to the brain. When paired with intentional breathwork, they can further stimulate the vagus nerve, a key player in helping us feel calm, clear, and regulated."

Ryan and I were recently discussing the science behind The Power of Gesture, specifically its connection to something called vagal tone. The vagus nerve is the longest cranial nerve in your body and plays a crucial role in your parasympathetic nervous system. Ryan explained that by activating this nerve—which gesture work can do—we may actually increase our longevity. **Science shows movement—like gesture—can lower the release of stress hormones such as cortisol, it can reduce heart rate, and increase heart rate variability—all signs of greater resilience and healing, which over time correlate with living a longer life.** And beyond all of what I just mentioned, gestures also bypass the thinking brain. They offer a way to process emotion through the body, not just through language. This is why so many people describe feeling "lighter," "clearer," "empowered," "like something shifted" after doing the practice.

Scientists like Gentilucci and Dalla Volta have also revealed that gestures and spoken language are processed in the same motor system of the brain, meaning hand movement is deeply tied to how we express and process emotion. When we move our bodies intentionally, we're not just going through motions—we're literally rewiring our relationship with our emotions, creating new neural pathways that allow us to access freedom and authenticity that our minds alone could never reach.

So the next time you feel something deeply in your body, remember: What you're feeling isn't just emotional—it's physiological. It's real. Your body holds profound wisdom that science is only beginning to understand. Through practices like The Power of Gesture, you're not fighting against your biology but rather partnering with it, allowing your body to do what it is designed to do: integrate your experiences, release what no longer serves you, and guide you back to wholeness.

This task can be hard because, in our culture, we're often taught to rely on our minds for the answers, while the body's wisdom takes a backseat. We are encouraged to *think* our way through things rather than *feel* our way through things. What a concept, right?

Let me explain. Feeling our way through life means tuning into the signals our body sends us—the sensations, emotions, and intuitive hits that show up before our mind even forms a thought. Do you ever have a gut feeling that something is off, even though you don't have any proof? Do you get goosebumps when something resonates deeply? Do you feel pulled toward someone without really understanding why? Those are examples of our body speaking. It's like we know something is right or needs to shift, but we are not sure exactly why or how.

On the other hand, thinking our way through things is about logic, where we rely on our minds to reason our way through things. While thinking is important for obvious reasons, it often overrides our emotional intelligence, dismissing the quiet wisdom our body is offering us. Feeling our way through life requires trust and an ability to slow down, go inward, and allow emotions to inform our decisions.

The challenge is that most of us haven't been taught how to listen to that intuition. In fact, from a young age, we're encouraged to prioritize logic and intellect—facts, scores, and external validation—over the subtle yet powerful messages from within. But imagine how different things could be if we were told early on that our body's wisdom is just as valuable as our mind's intellect.

What if, instead of searching for answers outside ourselves, we were encouraged to trust our internal guidance? What if we honored discomfort instead of ignoring it and allowed it to teach us? **The emotions you feel and the sensations they create are a result of your life experiences and are the exact right information you need to know what to do next.** These signals tell you what to hold on to, what to let go of, and when to start something new. Whether it's a career shift, a personal adventure, or a creative leap, your body knows the way.

9 KINDS OF INTELLIGENCE (ONLY ONE IS LOGICAL!)

Earlier, I shared my struggles related to intelligence and how it deeply impacted my life. This struggle continued well into adulthood, leaving me feeling inadequate and less-than. In my late twenties, I met a professor named Katie who introduced me to the work of Howard Gardner, a Harvard professor, psychologist, and author who has written a few dozen books on the many forms of intelligence.

Wait, what? There is more than one kind of intelligence? When I learned that there were multiple forms of intelligence, my heart burst open. I remember learning about this and feeling validated, seen and heard for the first time. I remember saying, almost in disbelief, "How did I not know this? How did I not know that there are many ways to learn, process, and express information? Why didn't my teachers tell me?" At first, I was in shock. Then, I experienced profound grief and sadness because I realized that for so many years, I thought something was wrong with me since I didn't fit into the narrow definition that society teaches us about what it means to be smart. I was just blown away. I had carried a secret, a heavy doubt that had me feeling small for so long. I kept asking, "How is this possible? How had I gone through life feeling less-than, just because I didn't fit into a one-size-fits-all way of learning?"

Then, a shift occurred. I thought, there had to be others that suffered just as I did. Almost immediately, I became grateful to realize a powerful truth: **There are many definitions of intelligence, ways to learn, and many ways to express our genius.** I dove into this research wholeheartedly. My 27 years of pain suddenly made sense.

Knowing that I could change the lives of so many with this information gave me a sense of purpose and a feeling of empowerment.

I developed a deep empathy for myself, which was extremely healing and eye-opening to the power of self-compassion. For the first time, I realized that the suffering I had carried for all of those years was not my fault. In order to hold on to the information being taught in school, I needed to touch, feel, and experience the lessons presented. My learning process relied on doing—using my body as a vehicle to learn—rather than passively hearing or seeing. Through my research, **I learned that this is known as kinesthetic intelligence, which refers to the ability to use our body effectively to express, solve problems, and create.** Individuals with this type of intelligence— many of whom are athletes, dancers, musicians, and surgeons—have a heightened awareness of physical movement, coordination, and the ability to manipulate objects skillfully. This term quickly became part of my vocabulary and shaped my deep understanding of the world we live in. Once I became enlightened with the research, my entire story shifted. I realized that I am not at all less than; in fact, I am more than I ever thought. This newfound understanding validated my existence in a way I had never experienced before, which literally altered the course of my life. I began to move through life with a confidence that was unfamiliar yet felt so right.

I was eager to absorb everything, to fill the academic voids that had lingered since school. When Katie, the professor, asked where I wanted to begin, I replied, "From the beginning." My thirst for knowledge traveled from politics and healthcare to nutrition and literature—I wanted to grasp it all. For five years, week by week, I would show up to her office with newspaper articles and ask to pair them with visuals from magazines. From there, I would create movements to represent the themes so that I could learn the lessons with my body. This wasn't anything I was taught. Having learned about kinesthetic intelligence was the information I needed to step into my learning style with confidence.

The world started to make sense. I began to comprehend and connect thoughts in a way that clicked for me. Mapping out ideas through movement gave me clarity—not just in learning but in how I valued myself. It boosted my confidence and made me feel capable and empowered. I broke free from a label that held me back for so long and began launching myself into the world, liberated and ready to take on what was coming next. For the first time, I was proud of who I was and how I learned.

When I share Howard Gardner's work on multiple forms of intelligence with my clients, I witness something extraordinary happen—it's like watching someone unlock a door they've been trying to open their whole life. Allow me to introduce you to Sarah.

When I first told Sarah, a client of mine, about Gardner's research, her whole body changed. She sat up straighter, took a deep breath, and said, "Wait, you mean the way I think, learn, and process information isn't wrong?" I could see that familiar moment when she realized nothing was wrong with her; instead, she was brilliant too, she had a talent to learn differently.

Sarah explained her struggle: "When I'm with creative people, I feel smart. I see and feel connection in such a deep way. But the moment I step into a meeting or a social gathering with analytical people, I shrink." She made herself smaller as she spoke, literally pulling inward. "I've spent years believing their opinion of me matters more than what I know to be true about myself."

I reflected what her body language was expressing as well as her words. Her body knew and was communicating without her having to think about it. She was blown away by this and after I asked her to embody this emotion, she simply continued from that place allowing her body to lead. Curling up into a ball, making herself as small as possible. Then I asked her to connect with her truth—that part of her that knows her creative intelligence is special, valuable, and powerful. "Now, let that truth transform this feeling," I invited.

After working with hundreds of people across diverse backgrounds and experiences, I've noticed a universal pattern: when we feel doubt, shame, worry, fear, and other limiting emotions, our gestures contract. We get small and shrink. On the other hand, when we feel empowered, alive, confident, capable, and worthy, our gestures expand. This is an awareness I want you to have because you can use this as a tool to shift your energy and emotions from what may feel limiting into what feels most empowering. Simple gestures can shift your entire experience and perspective.

What happened next took my breath away. She slowly began to unfold, extending her arms outward, reaching toward the sky. "Stand up," I encouraged. She rose, spreading her feet apart, arms stretching upward in a huge X formation—like a star reclaiming its brilliance. Tears streamed down her face. "I see it now," she said, her voice stronger than I'd ever heard it. "The only approval I need is my own. I've been treating my intelligence like something to apologize for instead of something to celebrate."

This is what happens when we understand that intelligence has many forms and that our unique "ways" in life have a place. Years of feeling "less than" begin to dissolve. Self-doubt transforms into self-trust. The parts of ourselves we've hidden become our greatest strengths.

Sarah created her own gestures that day—an anchor to return to whenever external voices try to make her small again. Now, when she starts to shrink in those analytical meetings or social gatherings, she can feel the X formation in her body and remember her form of intelligence doesn't need validation. It needs expression.

This transformation happens again and again. **Once we discover that our way of thinking, learning, and being in the world is valid—that there are many recognized forms of intelligence—everything shifts.**

We stop trying to fit into a mold that was never meant for us and start honoring our natural brilliance.

When we finally permit ourselves to learn, think, and create in the ways that feel natural to us, we don't just become more confident, we become more powerful, more authentic, and ultimately, more able to share our unique gifts with the world.

Imagine if, while learning in school, we were taught by experiencing the information instead of memorizing it—where learning wasn't just about absorbing facts and filling out multiple choice bubbles with a pencil, but truly embodying knowledge with our whole beings. For example, what if, while learning about geography, we molded our bodies into the shapes of states and countries? What if we felt the qualities of geography (i:e climate, temperature, water sources) by creating experiences where we could use all of our senses to learn? What if history lessons weren't just stories on a page, but interactive experiences that we felt in our body?

If we were taught from a young age to engage with our bodies as a tool for learning, there would be a good chance that we would not only view the body as a way to function but also as something we could rely on for guidance. Kinesthetic intelligence has inspired the development of The Power of Gesture in a very deep way, where we are able to integrate the body and mind, rebuild trust in ourselves, and lead our lives aligned and empowered.

I feel called to share a summary of Howard Gardner's theory here. My hope is that it will open something up for you, allowing you to consider how you view your own intelligence. In Gardner's book *Multiple Intelligences*, he focuses on nine forms of intelligence, which I will quickly define. In this book, I will be leaning heavily on kinesthetic, interpersonal, and intrapersonal; however, there are many forms worth exploring because you may find that you connect to several in different ways, which will absolutely empower your life.

1. **Bodily-Kinesthetic**: Coordination and physical skill.
2. **Interpersonal**: Understanding and interacting with others.
3. **Intrapersonal**: Self-awareness and introspection.
4. **Linguistic**: Sensitivity to language and the ability to use words effectively.
5. **Logical-Mathematical**: Skill in reasoning, logic, and problem-solving.
6. **Musical**: Ability to recognize and create musical patterns and rhythms.
7. **Spatial**: Capacity to think in three dimensions.
8. **Naturalistic**: Recognizing patterns in nature.
9. **Existential:** The ability to question human existence and the meaning of life.

What Gardner calls intrapersonal and interpersonal intelligence, Daniel Goleman, psychologist, author, and science journalist, calls emotional intelligence. Goleman breaks emotional intelligence down into these categories:

1. **Self-Awareness:** Recognizing your emotions as they arise and understanding how they affect your thoughts and actions.
2. **Self-Regulation:** Managing your emotions in a healthy way, staying in control, and adapting to situations without reacting impulsively.
3. **Motivation:** Having the drive to pursue goals with passion and resilience, fueled by inner values rather than external rewards.
4. **Empathy:** Understanding and sharing the feelings of others, which allows you to connect deeply and respond compassionately.
5. **Social Skills:** Building strong relationships, communicating effectively, and working well with others by navigating social dynamics gracefully.

Daniel Goleman's work shows that self-awareness, self-regulation, empathy, and social skills account for nearly 90 percent of what sets high performers apart. *Harvard Business Review* studies reveal that leaders with high EQ foster greater engagement, while TalentSmartEQ research shows that 90 percent of top performers exhibit high emotional intelligence compared to just 20 percent of low performers. I share this to underscore why this work matters deeply to your success as an embodied, empowered, and elevated leader in all aspects of your life.

Fun fact: **Research shows that our IQ, which is tied to our logical and mathematical skills, tends to peak in our twenties, whereas emotional intelligence, EQ, is not fixed and can be developed throughout our lives.** We have the ability to develop and deepen our intelligence—not just in the way we think but in the way we feel, make decisions, and engage with one another and in the world. This is exactly why The Power of Gesture is so transformative. By integrating kinesthetic and emotional intelligence, we create a practice that strengthens our ability to trust ourselves, process emotions, understand others, and make the right decisions for our lives. All of this translates into the power that already lives within us—that inner leader meant not only to guide us, but to guide others: our children, co-workers and teams. As we continue on, we will talk more about leadership from within and what that looks like when our self awareness deepens through this practice.

Our bodies have always known how to communicate in ways far beyond the spoken word. Before we learn to speak or understand complex topics, our bodies are already engaging with the world, feeling, responding, and connecting. This ancient form of communication—which we spoke about earlier—is something we all experience, but rarely acknowledge as something to rely on. I'm going to share a story of how I came to know this lesson in the most unexpected way.

LANGUAGE BEYOND WORDS

I met Sophie at sleepaway camp when I was 12. She was from France and came to the United States for the summer. From the moment we met, we were glued at the hip, inseparable. When camp ended, it was impossible to believe I wouldn't see her again until the next summer. It was hard for her as well, so instead of accepting that reality, she invited me to come to France after camp. My mom was hesitant to let a 12-year-old travel abroad alone, while my dad was confident about my abilities and somehow convinced my mom to let me go.

After visiting Paris, Sophie, her family, and I went to Corsica to vacation at their beach house. Her family was like no other. The cousins, aunts, uncles, and grandparents were endless, all moving through life with big energy and generosity on a level I had never experienced. Their passion was infectious, and their vibrancy was present in everything they did. Cooking was a multi-person activity. Boat rides on their yacht were filled with laughter. Everything they said and did was embedded with love. What struck me most was how the language barrier faded into the background. I may not have understood their spoken words, but I could feel their energy and warmth. Their body language, the tone of their voices, and the way they interacted with each other communicated volumes. This was one of the first experiences that taught me about connection beyond words.

Sophie's youngest brother, who was seven years old at the time, was one of the many who taught me this important lesson. I was drawn to him immediately and took to him like a sibling. Despite the lack of conversation and age difference, our connection was deep. We were buddies. We would play cards, laugh out loud, and hang out as if we'd known each other forever.

When it was time to return home, Sophie's family took me to the airport to board a small plane that would take me back to Paris before my flight to the United States. I remember sitting on the plane, look-ing at all of them, and waving goodbye out the airport window. Tears streamed down my face. How was it possible to connect with people so naturally and deeply without talking? This experience taught me the power of the body and how it speaks directly to our hearts and souls, bypassing the need for a single word. Truly amazing!

What if we were taught to trust the energy between two people, to feel it fully, and to recognize it as a form of intelligence that we could rely on without question? Our emotions aren't just fleeting sensations; they're information delivered directly to our bodies—wisdom we're meant to understand, learn from, and be guided by.

Through that experience along with some others, **I have come to learn that when we trust our body, we can access an entirely different dimension of human connection—one that transcends language, cultural barriers, and even spoken understanding.** Now let's turn inward and reconnect with this body wisdom that's been waiting for us all along.

HOW TO START LISTENING TO YOUR BODY

Knowing how powerful our bodies are and the deep truths they hold for us, I am sure you agree that the more tools we have to get to know ourselves, the better. It takes time to learn how to listen, understand, and ultimately trust the body's wisdom. However, I believe it's worth investing every single second because here's what becomes possible when you do:

- You get comfortable with your body's wisdom.
- You trust yourself and stop seeking answers outside of yourself.
- You are able to make bold decisions and stand by them because they are rooted in truth.

- You are able to communicate what it is you need with clarity and confidence.

Now that we know what's possible, let's explore some practical tools that will help you develop this connection beginning with the **6 Pillars of Awareness**—a framework I designed to help you reflect on your inner connection and identify areas where you can strengthen self-understanding. After that, we'll use an emotional tracking tool to build on that awareness. This tool will help you recognize your feelings and take steps to shift toward better-feeling ones. Finally, we'll transform this awareness into action through a philosophy I call **Embrace the Nudge**—an approach that helps us tune into feelings with a playful attitude and curiosity.

THE 6 PILLARS OF AWARENESS

1. SELF-DISCOVERY IS WHEN YOU TAKE THE TIME TO UNDERSTAND YOURSELF AND ALIGN WITH WHAT TRULY MATTERS TO YOU.

How to Use: Ask yourself: *Do I stand for what I truly believe?* If yes, that's amazing because you know yourself well enough to trust and believe in how you really feel. If your answer is no, that is excellent information to have. Here is my suggestion: Write a list of five values that are most important to you (e.g., honesty, creativity, connection, respect, compassion). Reflect on one decision you made in the past week and ask: *Did this decision align with my values?* If yes, write how making that aligned choice made you feel; if no, write honestly about why. Were you afraid, intimidated, or not ready? Writing honestly will give you a sense about what you will want to pay attention to.

2. SELF-ACCEPTANCE IS WHEN YOU EMBRACE WHO YOU ARE, NOT ONLY YOUR STRENGTHS, BUT YOUR STRUGGLES AS WELL.

How to Use: Write one struggle and one strength and then combine them to create an empowering affirmation. Here are some examples:

- **Struggle:** "I am finding it hard to be present."
- **Strength:** "I am a good listener."
- **Affirmation:** "I honor the present moment by listening deeply to myself and those around me."

- **Struggle:** "I compare myself to others."
- **Strength:** "I love to have a good time."
- **Affirmation:** "I celebrate my unique journey and focus on creating joy in my own life."

- **Struggle:** "I need constant connection."
- **Strength:** "I enjoy my alone time."
- **Affirmation:** "I find clarity in my time alone."

3. SELF-REFLECTION IS WHERE YOU PRACTICE GOING INWARD AND GETTING QUIET ENOUGH TO FEEL AND HEAR WHAT EMOTIONS SHOW UP.

How to Use: At the end of the day, write a journal entry in response to: "*What experience stood out today? What emotions did I feel during that experience? What could I do differently tomorrow to support myself even more?*"

4. SELF-CARE IS WHEN YOU NURTURE YOUR PHYSICAL, EMOTIONAL, AND MENTAL HEALTH TO CREATE BALANCE AND A STRONGER CONNECTION TO HAPPINESS.

How to Use: Write an intention for self-care this week. Start with: "*This week, I will nurture myself by…*" List one actionable step (i.e., taking a 10-minute walk, preparing a healthy meal, journaling before bed) and schedule it in your calendar. I find this helps me and my clients ensure that the goal happens.

5. SELF-EMPOWERMENT IS TAKING CONTROL OF YOUR LIFE BY MAKING CHOICES, EVEN IF THEY ARE HARD.

How to Use: Identify an area of your life where you feel stuck or disempowered. It could be anything from a personal relationship, a career decision, or a habit you're struggling with. For example:

- If you've been avoiding a difficult conversation with your boss about a promotion, your actionable step might be: "Today, I will schedule a 15-minute meeting with my boss to discuss my career path."
- If you feel powerless in a friendship where your boundaries aren't respected, your step could be: "I will practice saying 'no' to one request that doesn't align with my energy today."
- If you're struggling with self-care, your action might be: "I will block out 20 minutes this evening for myself, even if it means passing on other obligations."

Once you have that action written down, and have made a commitment to follow through with it, finish by using this affirmation to support yourself: "*I trust my choices and honor my truth with every action I take.*"

6. SELF-ACTUALIZATION IS WHEN YOU ARE LIVING IN ALIGNMENT WITH YOUR HIGHEST TRUTH.

How to Use: Reflect on what "living my highest truth" means to you. Write a vision statement beginning with: *"When I am fully aligned, I…"* Include what is working for you so that you can reinforce that and identify what you want to prioritize and how you want to show up in the world.

When I am fully aligned, I move through my day with calm confidence. I prioritize morning time for myself before diving into work. I speak honestly in meetings, even when it feels vulnerable. I create boundaries around my energy and say no when activities don't feel right in my body. I listen to my need for rest without guilt. I trust that my creative ideas have value and share them without apology. I am present with my family rather than distracted by my phone. When challenges arise, I pause to feel before reacting.

The Six Pillars are designed for you to see where you are currently and where you may have more work to do. You may realize that you don't have a consistent self-care ritual and would like one, or you might feel you are too hard on yourself and need to work more on self-acceptance. Once you have this awareness of yourself, you can start to take action from that place. This isn't about shame or feeling like you are not doing enough; it's simply about continuing the commitment to become more deeply aware so that you can become the best version of yourself.

TRACKING YOUR EMOTIONS

Now that we have aligned our awareness with the six pillars and have identified where we can spend a little bit more time, we are going to be able to track our emotions more easily. Inspired by Abraham Hicks' Emotional Guidance Scale, I developed **The Alignment Ladder** to give you a clear path toward feeling better. This practice invites you to notice your current emotional state and gently reach for a better feeling. I say the word "gently" intentionally because it is meant to be gentle. Just like climbing a ladder, progress happens step by step, not in one giant leap. Each emotion becomes a stepping stone toward how you ultimately want to feel, which will get you into the proper alignment. **By observing how you feel, you can notice patterns and identify opportunities for growth, navigating where you want to go next.**

For example, moving from fear to anger might not seem like progress but it is. Anger has energy and momentum that fear lacks. While fear can leave you feeling paralyzed, anger can inspire action or the courage to create change. Similarly, moving from disappointment to contentment may feel small, but it's significant. Disappointment keeps you stuck in unmet expectations, while contentment offers acceptance, creating space for new possibilities to show up.

Below is a list of 10 sets of emotions, each representing a step on the ladder. Imagine you're standing on the bottom step (Step 10), looking up. Ask yourself, "What's a better feeling I can aim for? What feels realistic for me right now?" Each step up is a positive one, bringing you closer to feelings like joy, appreciation, and love. There's no need to rush, but a little push can help. Here's a specific example: if you're carrying anger from a work incident into your home life, take a moment before bed to reflect on this feeling. Acknowledge your anger, then consciously choose to shift to a slightly lighter emotion, such as frustration. It's not joy, but it's a lighter energy that will make you feel better while acknowledging that you are, in fact, making progress. The goal is to choose the next best feeling and let the momentum build naturally. Step by step, you'll reclaim your energy and rise into alignment. Let's start climbing!

THE ALIGNMENT LADDER

1. **Empowered/Joy/Appreciation/Love:** A state of alignment and fullness.
2. **Passion/Excitement:** Energy and drive to take inspired action.
3. **Enthusiasm/Eagerness:** A hopeful feeling of momentum to move forward.
4. **Optimism/Belief:** Trust in positive outcomes and seeing what is possible.
5. **Contentment:** Feeling grounded and peaceful.
6. **Frustration/Irritation:** Feeling blocked but motivated to move forward.
7. **Disappointment/Discouragement:** Feeling setbacks but not defeated.
8. **Anger:** A surge of energy to address what's wrong.
9. **Insecurity/Worry:** Feeling uncertain and concerned.
10. **Fear/Grief/Despair:** Feeling stuck or powerless.

EMBRACING THE NUDGE

Now that we understand the ladder, let's start deepening our awareness around how we feel so that we can make the decision to feel even better when we need to.

Do any of these sound familiar?

- **You're in a meeting, and someone asks a question you weren't prepared for:** Your heart pounds as you hesitate to give an answer.
- **You are about to have a conversation that you have been dreading but know you need to have it:** Your chest tightens and your breath feels shallow.

- **You're carrying stress from a long day, overwhelmed by work, and it feels like the weight of the world is on your back:** Your shoulders feel heavy.
- **You run into someone you haven't seen in a long time:** You smile and give them a hug.
- **You overhear a conversation that you know you shouldn't:** Your stomach drops.
- **You hear a song that reminds you of a beautiful memory:** Warmth fills your chest, and goosebumps appear on your arms.
- **You are having an intimate moment with your partner:** Your mind is distracted, and your body is just moving through the motions.

These nudges are the sensations your body gives you in response to emotional reactions. It's your body speaking to you, trying to tell you that something matters, something is off, something is right or something needs to shift. Listening to these nudges may feel unfamiliar or awkward at first, but it's that deeper understanding we need to align with so we can make a choice of how many steps we need to take.

Here are some more common nudges our bodies might give us to communicate. I have categorized them and added what the nudges may be associated with so you can start to make those connections more easily.

STRESS OR DISCOMFORT NUDGES

Tight shoulders or neck: Stress, worry or overwhelm.
Grinding teeth: Suppressed anger, frustration, or anxiety.
Tightness in the chest: Grief, sadness, or suppressed emotions.

GUT REACTION NUDGES

Butterflies in the stomach: Excited or nervous.
Nausea: Rejection, or misalignment
Gut dropping/sinking: Warning, danger, or dread

PHYSICAL NUDGES

Goosebumps or chills: Truth, resonance, or recognition
Restlessness: Change, movement, or action
Sudden energy surge: Excitement, alignment, danger

Now that we have the **6 pillars of awareness** to check in with, the alignment ladder to set a goal where we want to go, and the embracing the nudge tool to support us on our journey, we have a framework to follow, a path with supported tools. You can find worksheets to print out and track your progress at www.jenaks.com/yourbodyisspeaking

YOU HAVE THE AWARENESS, NOW WHAT?

Now that we know that these nudges aren't just random physical sensations—that they're our body's intelligence speaking directly to us for guidance, let's take it a step further. What if we used that guidance as a tool to create a strong foundation for one of the most important aspects of self-care: creating healthy boundaries—where we decide what we will allow into our body—and I don't mean food or drink. I mean energy. Each time you allow someone to speak to you unkindly, tell you that you are something you're not, or share a depressing story, low-vibe energy enters your body, sits there, and can manifest into more of the same. I'm not saying every conversation has this quality. What I am saying is that when it does, you have the ability and the right to decide how long you engage and when it is time to leave.

Setting boundaries isn't always easy because it requires us to have honest and uncomfortable conversations with people, some of whom we love. However, it's exactly what we need to do in order to stay in alignment and feel empowered. This phase of becoming embodied is partly about taking your power back by deciding what you want and what you don't, regardless of what others think.

Creating boundaries can sometimes feel like we're doing something wrong because not everyone will like what we have to say. It's okay. We want to move away from people-pleasing and lean into what we truly want to be doing with our time and energy. If that means no longer spending time with people who don't make you happy, then do it. If that means creating a boundary with someone because what they say causes you to feel anxious, scared, or sad, then do it. If that means telling your friend, partner, or boss that when they speak to you in a certain tone, it upsets you, then do it. AND, if it means making extra plans with people that lift you up, that's not just "allowed"—it's essential. Your energy is precious, your time is limited, and investing both in relationships that make you feel alive is one of the most powerful forms of self-care you can practice.

The story I'm about to share is a personal one—a boundary moment—where I had to decide if I would give my power away to a cultural expectation or if I would stand in my truth, even if it meant shaking things up a bit.

Maybe you've experienced something like this yourself—a time where you felt torn between doing what was expected and honoring the voice within. Perhaps there was a time when you didn't find the strength to step forward, yet wanted to. That's okay. **We all face moments when fear or doubt holds us back, I certainly have. I share this story not to judge those moments, but to illuminate what becomes possible when we allow ourselves to trust that inner knowing.**

CHOOSING INTUITION OVER TRADITION

Parenting from within, guided by intuition, has always felt like an authentic path for me, yet also isolating. Especially in my kids' younger years, it was challenging to navigate external pressures and unsolicited opinions when, deep down, I knew many of those influences didn't align with my own.

Almost immediately after my son was born, it was time for his circumcision, a traditional practice in the Jewish religion where a small piece of skin, called the foreskin, is removed from a baby boy's penis shortly after birth. Circumcision is often done for cultural or religious reasons. Some believe it has health benefits, while others see it as a tradition. We did it mostly for tradition, and because it was what was familiar.

I remember our friends and family filling up our apartment and ready to celebrate. Tradition said that I should stay back—that mothers step away while fathers and Rabbis comfort the baby during the circumcision. But here's the thing about body wisdom: it doesn't care about "shoulds" or tradition.

As I stood against the far windows, a strong feeling moved through me—a surge of maternal energy so powerful it literally pushed me off the wall. Before my mind could catch up with all the reasons I should stay put, my body was already in motion, carrying me straight to my son. Without hesitation, I found myself right beside him, locking eyes, making sure he knew I was there too.

In that moment, I wasn't just challenging tradition—I was honoring something deeper. Something primal. The wisdom in my cells that knew exactly where I needed to be. This was one of my son's first gifts to me—teaching me that if I want to live an honest life, when my body speaks with that kind of clarity, listening isn't optional. It's essential.

This lesson my son taught me raises an important question: Why does involving the body matter so much in our journey toward empowerment?

Bessel van der Kolk's work shows us that our bodies literally "keep the score" of our experiences. Think about it—all those traditions, expectations, and "shoulds" we follow without question don't just live in our minds. They're stored in our physical being—in how our shoulders tense up at family gatherings, how our throats tighten when we consider speaking our truth, or how our stomachs knot when we're about to break from the norm.

In that moment with my son, my body wasn't just having a reaction—it was speaking its wisdom, cutting through generations of stored tradition and programming. My body was saying, "This doesn't align with what feels true for you," and before I allowed my mind to get in the way, I trusted the guidance from within.

When we honor these bodily signals, we don't just make better choices in the moment; we begin to heal the disconnect between who we've been told to be and who we truly are. This is exactly what van der Kolk means when he says our bodies keep the score—they remember everything and are always trying to guide us home to ourselves.

When I reflect on the story above, I remember an empowering tool I used and will share it with you now. We've all heard about positive affirmations, right? But here's what most people miss: when words stay just in your head, they often don't stick. **Embodied affirmations are different—they're a powerful tool that combines what you say with how you move, creating a full-body experience that actually rewires your nervous system.**

Here's why this works: Your body and brain are in constant conversation. When you pair an affirmation like "I am strong" with a physical gesture—standing tall with your chest open and arms wide—your body actually sends signals to your brain that match the words. This creates a feedback loop that makes the affirmation feel real.

The simplest way to practice this is by using The Power of Gesture bodyset. Place one hand over your heart, the other on your belly, close your eyes, and say "I trust myself" while feeling the warmth of your hands on your body. Now try extending your arms outward, palms facing the sky, in a releasing motion while saying "I let go of what's not mine to carry." Hold there for a moment. Feel the release. Now, bring your hands back to your body, one hand on your heart and one hand on your belly. Repeat the affirmation "I trust myself". Hold that gesture and feel the energy once again. I invite you to move back and forth between the release of what no longer serves you and the return to your body to feel into the trust.

My hope is that by now you are seeing what an ally your body truly is. That it's here to guide you, inform you and protect you. Here's a short story where my body's guidance saved my life.

MY BODY TO THE RESCUE

In my teenage years, dance became my sanctuary, a safe place that I could always retreat to. As an adult, I always loved going to dance clubs alone, weaving through the crowd, dancing both alone and together, often wearing a baseball or cowboy hat with a large brim because it allowed me to feel like I was in my own world. Private or public, it was me feeling free. Dance was much more than movement. It was a connection that transcended words into a language that I could understand. I quickly learned that this universal language was not only a way to connect and understand the world but was also a tool that helped me realign with the power inside of me. Dance took me out of my head, where my self-doubt lived, and into my body, where my self-worth was being discovered. Movement allowed me to feel grounded in my body, powerful in my presence, and honest in my expression. It was as though every time I danced—on a stage, on the street, in a club, or in my home—I was having a reunion with my soul, which ultimately helped me remember who I was.

Our bodies are not only vehicles to tap into joy, liberation and connection, they can also be our greatest protectors. If it wasn't for my body speaking to me, I would most definitely be a statistic of rape. At 25 years old, I was heading to an appointment in midtown Manhattan. I walked into a building where my meeting was being held and entered an empty elevator, or so I thought. When I turned around, I saw that a man had slipped in without me noticing. He began with a stare, and made his way toward me. He asked my name. I ignored him at first until I realized that he wasn't going to stop until I answered. I finally said quietly, "Jen." I tried to mind my own business, but before I knew it, he pulled the security knob on the elevator, which then came to a stop. There was no alarm because the building was old and a bit run down. He got in my face, staring at me intensely, and my body began to shake. No one knew where I was. There were no cameras to track and no service on my phone, no one was coming; I was terrified. He started touching my body, everywhere. On top of my shirt, over my breasts, and between my legs. My head felt hot, I was scared and said to myself, *This is it, I am going to be raped.*

Before I knew it, something so big, way beyond logical reasoning or decision-making, came through me. My body lifted with confidence and I said, "My apartment is on the seventh floor." The truth? My appointment was on the seventh floor. "It would be nice to have a bed, don't you think?" It truly was like an out-of-body experience. I had no idea where that confidence and words came from. Immediately, his energy shifted. It was almost like watching a balloon poked and deflated. I could see the confusion rushing through him. I think he wanted the resistance, the fight but my body knew better and guided me. He pushed the knob back in, and off we went up to the seventh floor. When we got off of the elevator, he wouldn't let me go.

I saw the office for my appointment, broke free and ran. I quickly opened the door, slammed it behind me and started to scream and cry. The assistant ran after the guy but it was too late, he was gone.

Even when fear or angst is at its most heightened, when heat is rushing through the body, our bodies know how to stand strong and inform us of what we need. I'm going to remind you of something I said at the beginning of the book because it relates to the story I just shared and acts as a great reminder for all of us.

Humans have always relied on the body's natural intelligence for survival, our ancestors trusted their instincts to sense danger, find safety, and navigate the unknown. A quickened heartbeat warned of predators, tense muscles signaled readiness, and intuition guided crucial decisions. This deep connection to the body was essential to life itself. But as society evolved, we prioritized logic over intuition and external validation over internal truth and became disconnected from this innate wisdom. Today, in a world filled with distractions and fear-based narratives, many of us ignore the subtle cues of our bodies when we need them the most. Those signals, the guidance we seek, are still within us, waiting to be heard. Reconnecting with our bodies isn't just returning to something ancient; it's a vital act of self-trust, and we need it now more than ever.

LET'S SUMMARIZE WHAT WE KNOW

1. **Intelligence Goes Beyond Logic and Math:** Research shows that kinesthetic and emotional intelligence are measurable forms of intelligence that influence decision-making and self-awareness. Developing these intelligences builds resilience in ways traditional education often overlooks.

2. **Our Emotions Are Powerful Teachers**: Neuroscience confirms that emotions carry information that help us make choices aligned with our highest self.

3. **The Body Stores Emotional Memories**: van der Kolk's research proves that emotions live in our bodies, not just our minds. Embodied practices access these stored patterns which create neurological changes that thought-based approaches alone cannot achieve.

Awakening Your Emotional & Kinesthetic Intelligence

With this **Power of Gesture** exercise, we're going to reconnect with that ancient yet familiar and natural intelligence within us so that we can deepen our self trust and remember how to rely on our body's wisdom first—before someone else's. I'm going to modify it here; however, you can experience a longer version by scanning the QR code at the end of this chapter or by visiting www.jenaks. com/yourbodyisspeaking, where you will find The Power of Gesture chapter videos. Press play, and I will be there to guide you through the experience.

STEP 1: INTENTION

Find a comfortable spot and take a moment to bodyset, or just listen to my voice. Close your eyes, place one hand on your heart and one hand on your belly. Take a few deep breaths and say the following intention either in your mind or out loud: "I open myself to the wisdom of my Emotional and Kinesthetic Intelligence, allowing my hand gestures to reveal insights my mind may not be able to access."

STEP 2: IDENTIFY

While your eyes are closed, allow your mind to take you to a memory where you suppressed an instinct you had because you doubted yourself or were afraid of what others would think. While you recall that moment, allow yourself to experience the feeling.

1. Name your moment.
2. Notice how it makes you feel.
3. Notice where you feel it in your body.

STEP 3: GESTURE #1: EMBODY

Use the information you just gathered to help you create your first gesture. Notice the quality of the emotion—is it restricting? Allow your hands to move in a way that connects to that feeling. Some examples could be exhaustion, so your shoulders get heavy and your hands might rest there with weight. Overwhelm could be felt in the jaw, so your hands hold your jaw with some pressure. Or possibly, disconnection is felt in the throat, and the hands embody a gesture representing a closing off.

STEP 4: IDENTIFY

Now, see yourself in a memory or an imagined experience where you are expressing yourself fully. Trusting yourself. Opening up completely, unapologetically. Believing in your instincts.

1. Name the emotion.
2. Notice how it makes you feel.
3. Notice where you feel it in your body.

STEP 5: GESTURE #2: EMBODY

Use this information to create your second gesture. Maybe you are opening your heart with a sense of expansiveness and giving yourself the opportunity to feel the power of your strength. It's there. It always has been. Allow yourself to feel it.

STEP 6: INTEGRATE

Integrate both gestures by moving back and forth from the restriction to the expansion a couple of times, allowing the emotional duality to teach you something you may not have known about yourself.

TIPS FOR GESTURE PRACTICE

- **Bodyset:** Place one hand on your heart, one hand on your belly, and close your eyes.
- **Move slowly**: Allow yourself to express and listen to what your body is saying.
- **Repeat:** Repetition gives the body more time to process and communicate.
- **Music:** Choose a piece of music that inspires you.

STEP 7: JOURNAL

I invite you to document how your body feels after the practice and reflect on any new realizations that may have been made.

Remember, the intelligence of your body goes beyond emotions—your movement patterns, physical responses, and gestures hold wisdom your thinking mind can't access alone. When you honor both Emotional and Kinesthetic Intelligence, you reclaim a powerful internal guidance system that helps you navigate life with greater alignment and authenticity.

> **Empowered Affirmation:** *"I trust the wisdom that moves through my hands and heart, honoring both what I feel and what my body knows."*

Ready to dive deeper? This QR code will take you to
The Power of Gesture: Awakening Your Emotional &
Kinesthetic Intelligence video, where you'll join me for a full
immersive experience that brings these concepts to life.

PART TWO
EMPOWER

EMPOWER IS ABOUT ACTION AND OWNERSHIP fueled by a strong, aligned foundation where values, desires, and empowering stories stack up to reflect who you are and what truly matters to you. This phase is about embracing all parts of you, owning them and taking inspired action in your life.

If you are questioning whether or not you have arrived at the empower phase, I invite you to reflect back on some of the exercises that you completed in Part 1: Embody. There is a lot of benefit in continuing to reflect because, while something may not have clicked the first time, it may click the second, third, or fourth. An important part of this entire exploration is to know that the embody, empower, and elevate journey is a cycle. It's a cycle that expects you to circle back because it mirrors the natural flow of life. For example, you may feel like you have mastered embody, and then once halfway through the empower phase, lose your grip again, start self-doubting and become out of alignment. It's okay. Remembering that we are not meant to stay stagnant is important. We're human, life happens and throws us off track. Life's a cycle and so are the 3 E's. This level of acceptance creates space for constant growth because we not only move through lifewith more ease, we know that each stage provides learning opportunities, which inevitably help us elevate even more.

I have to share something that truly lights me up inside! You know the feeling when two powerful ideas come together in a way that suddenly makes both of them even more meaningful? That's what happened when I realized how beautifully the two teachings I'm about to share with you align. It's so powerful. I have to share them with you now.

Neville Goddard, a spiritual teacher and author known for his work on the power of imagination and manifestation, says, "Assume the feelings of the wish fulfilled." This perspective so beautifully complements Stephen Covey's wisdom that we explored in Chapter 1 to "Begin with the end in mind." While Covey encourages us to envision our destination clearly, Goddard takes us a step further—inviting us to not just see that destination but to feel it in our bodies as if it's already happened. This means that if you want to make your desires a reality, you need to embody the state of having already achieved your desire, aligning the emotions and thoughts as if your wish were already fulfilled. When we give ourselves permission to feel how we want to feel right now—not someday—we naturally stay aligned with the 3 E's cycle longer.

WHY DOES IT MATTER?

When you are empowered, you're ready—ready to create a plan and take action toward the things you've been avoiding. At this point, you've developed a strong awareness that allows you to recognize when you're slipping out of alignment and may need to use The Power of Gesture to get you back on track. There's a newfound sense of freedom as your need for external validation diminishes, replaced by self-trust. **Feeling empowered brings a smile to your face because**

you're returning home to who you truly are, believing deeply that what you want to create is possible. Living empowered means living your truth—and there's simply no better feeling than that.

HOW WILL IT IMPROVE YOUR LIFE?

Feeling empowered transforms how we move through the world. Suddenly, we're breaking free from old limitations and taking full ownership of our choices. The foundation we've built during the embody phase now supports everything making challenges feel manageable. Difficult conversations and high-pressure situations no longer derail you because you're speaking and acting from alignment. This steady confidence creates a positive momentum—each empowered choice supporting energy for the next one. The path ahead feels good, even when it's challenging, because you know you're leading your life from a place of truth, and as a result, you attract opportunities that are aligned with the life you're creating.

As we move through the empower phase, I invite you to remember that authentic expression is not only good for us—it creates ripple effects that positively impact everyone around us. Your truth is not just a gift to yourself but to the world.

In chapter three, we'll explore techniques to deepen self connection so that even when life throws a curve ball, you'll know how to find your way back home. You'll learn to establish healthy boundaries, stand firmly in your truth, and move through life with a newfound confidence. This phase is about breaking free from outside influences, staying true to your path, and stepping fully into personal power. The path to feeling empowered begins with the courage to be authentically you. You have already taken that step by being here, so let's get started.

CHAPTER 3

BREAKING FREE FROM CONFORMITY: EMPOWERING OUR TRUTH

Surrender isn't giving up; it's rising up, living elevated,
and embracing the fullness of what is meant for you.

How do we break free from the rules and expectations we were taught so we can lead our lives from within and fully embody our truth? Throughout our journey together, we've explored the importance of becoming embodied, turning inward, and using our emotions as guides to live authentically. Now, I invite you to embrace the concept of permission, allowing yourself the freedom to explore, empowering yourself to express fully, and embracing whatever shows up.

GIVING YOURSELF PERMISSION

Permission to trust our intuition, even when it feels risky; to rewrite the narrative that's been told to us and create one that resonates with our truth; to take up space; to be unapologetically seen and heard; to prioritize joy and release the guilt for doing so; and to embrace the message because it's an invitation to be fully human.

Giving ourselves permission isn't always an easy thing to do. Sometimes, it takes a good friend saying, "It's okay," before we can take that step. But what I have come to believe is that life gives us permission slips all the time. Those quiet and unexpected moments— they're often invitations to step more fully into who we truly are.

I'm going to share a story with you that changed everything for me. At first, it seemed like just another challenging moment—the kind we all face. But looking back, I realize it was actually a profound doorway into freedom. This experience became my template for what it looks like to live unapologetically in my truth, no matter what opinions or traditions stood in my way.

It happened with my parents, who, without even realizing it, opened a door that would shape my future and transform how I move through the world. Their unintentional permission slip became one of my greatest teachers.

As you read, I invite you to reflect on your own life and contemplate what quiet lessons might have been placed in front of you without your awareness. What moments, big or small, may have been teaching you something profound about permission and living authentically? It's never too late to notice them because these lessons remain within you, ready to be rediscovered in a new way, and used as tools to guide your truth.

MY MOM, THE NONCONFORMIST

I was eight when my parents divorced, and my mom suddenly found herself raising three kids on her own while juggling multiple jobs. In my teens and certainly, as I became an adult, I realized that my mom's actions spoke volumes and taught me more than any classroom or book series ever could. My mom's life is a living testament to the principles of family, work ethic and authentic connection. Her example continues to shape, inform and give me the courage to live my truth every single day.

I clearly remember the day my parents told my brothers and me that their marriage was over. That moment isn't just a memory; it lives in my body still. When I reflect on that moment, as I am now, I can still feel and see it all. I was sitting on a patterned green and yellow couch with my mom, facing my two brothers, who were sitting across from us. My dad was at the head of the room in what I remember to be another patterned chair. It was the 70s, so everything was a bit funky back then, which I loved.

I remember our outfits, which I also still love to this day—plaid pants and shirts, our somewhat wild, untamed hair. I was eight, my middle brother was 11, and my oldest brother was 15. I remember holding my mom's hand, not fully understanding what was happening, but sensing that something serious was about to unfold.

They told us they were getting divorced. The experience was emotional yet awkwardly calm at the same time. I knew this was important but didn't realize how much things were about to shift. It was just a couple of hours later when I was in my brother's room playing music and asked everyone to come in. I remember trying to bring my parents together through dancing. I grabbed their hands, placed them together, and as quickly as I brought their hands together, they dropped them, one and then the other. Life had changed, and that was that. We began visiting my dad on weekends while living with our mom during the week. This marked the beginning of many lessons, all leading to the realization that living your truth sometimes requires difficult choices and might mean hurting the ones you love.

My mother continued to be an incredible example in my life. She is a fighter, a survivor, someone who has always worked hard in life. She stands in her power with courage, bravery, and honesty, qualities I deeply admire and still pay close attention to. While raising me and my brothers, she worked multiple jobs and got up every morning to swim at the YMCA beforehand. My mom would take me with her and have me sit on the couch on the second floor of the YMCA. There were floor-to-ceiling glass windows which allowed me to see the pool and watch her swim laps. She needed that time for herself, and because of that, **I learned how important that type of time is. Alone time. Thinking time. Clear your mind and strengthen your body time.** It is truly amazing how I can feel the experience as I write this. I can feel the energy that I felt looking at this woman who I so admired doing what she needed to do to have inner peace, balance, focus, and clarity in her own life.

My mother taught me how to stand strong in the face of adversity, live truthfully, and honor yourself no matter what. She taught me that if I want to walk a path that seems unconventional or lonely, it doesn't mean it's wrong; in fact, it could be the exact right thing. She taught me to listen to my intuition and trust its guidance—to know that if I felt something, it was real and to never doubt it, no matter what.

One of the earliest lessons I learned about intuition and the body's wisdom came from observing my mom's approach to our health. She raised the three of us during a time when resources and guidance weren't nearly as accessible as they are now. She didn't have the luxury of the internet or immediate responses from professionals. Instead, she had to rely on her instincts. I vividly remember how she would assess our temperature by placing her warm cheek on our foreheads, bypassing the need for a thermometer. That connection—the heat between two bodies—gave her the information she needed to make important decisions. This small gesture had a significant impact on my life. I would wonder how she could be so confident in trusting the signals her body received to guide her choices with our health. That was a lasting imprint that lives with me to this day.

MY MOM'S LESSONS TO ME (AND YOU!)

- Empowerment starts with honoring your truth. Let it be your guiding light, and if it leads you to break free from conformity, trust that it's the path you're meant to take.
- Alone time isn't just a luxury—it's essential. Use it to reset, realign, and remember who you truly are and what you need.
- Your body holds deep wisdom. Pay attention to its signals, and never give your power away.

Thanks, Mom!

YOUR UNAPOLOGETIC TRUTH IS A GIFT

Do these sound familiar? *Crying is weak. Laughing out loud is too bold. Kissing on the street is rude. Dancing in public is odd. Don't take up too much space. Being emotional means you're out of control. Speaking up makes you difficult. Celebrating yourself is arrogant. Letting go means you don't care.*

Here is what I have learned: **Authenticity is power, and when you show up as powerful, it can cause discomfort in others and make them feel insecure.** Raw honesty and vulnerability are often unfamiliar and unsettling to many. So instead, they make comments to try to make you feel smaller to make themselves feel bigger. But here's what I have realized: When you remain true to who you are—whether that means crying when you're sad, laughing hysterically at something no one else finds funny, kissing someone you love at the most random time—you are not only honoring your truth, you are giving the world a gift. You become a teacher, a guide, and an inspiration. You are now giving other people permission to be authentic, offering them the permission they might not yet have given themselves.

I recently had a session with a client that absolutely blew my mind. Gabby came from a very conservative, deeply religious household and community. From day one, she was told what to wear, what to say, how to behave—and was married off at 16 years old. She never had a chance to find her own voice or her own path. Passion was not allowed. In fact, when any version of it was expressed, it was looked at as a sin. She explained that growing up, joy was not allowed to be indulged because it would "take away a huge portion of the eternal joy." Her world was not meant to be enjoyed; it was meant to be enslaved for God so one could acquire as much paradise as possible. Joy, she was taught, was a vain thing in this world. You were only to rejoice in serving God. Nothing else.

When Gabby first sat down with me, she described how all of her conditioning had piled on top of her head like a tower of pressure, pressing down to fit that mold. "My body feels so heavy, unheard, unseen," she said. "I have this roaring energy that feels like it's banging on an iron door trying to get out." She looked at me with desperate eyes. "I have always been confused because I cannot understand— without this ingredient, how can we survive life? I know I need joy, but how do I access it?" I explained that joy was within her—but to access it, we first needed to allow her anger to express itself. I asked her where she felt this trapped energy in her body. As I put on instrumental music, she paused, closed her eyes, and connected with her bodyset. 'My heart, chest, and belly feel like they're going to explode,' she said. Her gestures started small—hands squished together, creating pressure and stillness. Then she progressed to fists banging against her thighs. After a couple of minutes, I could see in her face that there was so much to release that these small movements weren't enough. She had to fully embody the gestures. "Stand up," I invited her. "Let your whole body join in."

Before I knew it, she was jumping, kicking, punching—letting it all out. And then, within a couple of minutes, something extraordinary happened. A smile so big, so beautiful, came to her face and her body softened in the movement. It was incredible to witness. **Her hands were unclenched. Her chest raised. Her movements transformed from rage into flow. I was in awe and excitement, watching as she allowed her body to speak and lead the way.**

When the song ended, she stood there with tears streaming down her face. Gabby had found joy. Liberation came from permission. She had given anger a voice, allowed it to express itself, and then freedom arrived to feel the joy. She broke free with the gestures, giving herself the opportunity to rage. "I punctured a hole in the balloon," she said, "I needed to rip it open and allow all of the joy to come out—and it did."

When Gabby returned for our next session, she shared how several of her friends had commented that her face seemed "lit up" that week. They were very curious about the shift in her. "They want what I have now," she said. "They can see it, even if they don't know what 'it' is."

What struck me most was her understanding that her healing had created an opening—not just for herself but for others in her community. By allowing her body to speak its truth, she had become a living example of what's possible. Her courage to break free was silently giving others the permission slip they needed to question their own constraints and find their own path to joy.

Trusting our body may seem like a foreign concept because it's not often taught; however, it is the most important practice of our life. This is where our wisdom and power lie—in those moments when we choose to let our emotions move through us rather than trap them inside.

When we silence what needs expression, we're not just hiding from the world—we're hiding from ourselves. Those unexpressed emotions don't disappear. They settle into our muscles, tighten our jaws, knot our stomachs, and create a heaviness that we carry every-where. This is what creates the weight that can make us feel stuck, disconnected, and small.

Here's what I've learned through my own journey and witnessed with my clients: Your authentic expression isn't just about you. When you allow yourself to cry that cry, rage that rage, or dance that dance, you become an example for others. You're now living proof that it's safe to feel, safe to be real, safe to take up space. **Your courage to express becomes someone else's permission slip to do the same.**

Gabby's story shows us that joy and anger aren't opposites—they're partners. When we embrace this concept, we know that we might need to punch through the wall of anger before we can access the freedom on the other side. The Power of Gesture gives us a way to do this safely, to let our bodies speak what our words cannot, to transform trapped energy into liberated movement.

I want to say something to you right here, right now, with strong conviction and passion: When you are unsettled about something, there is a reason. When you are scared, there is a reason. When you are sad, don't doubt it! When you are laughing your ass off, and no one else is, keep laughing. This is your body speaking. It is your truth coming out, and honestly, there is nothing more beautiful than that! Don't ever let anyone take that away from you.

In *The Body Keeps The Score*, Bessel van der Kolk says: "Neurosci-ence research shows that the only way we can change the way we feel is by becoming aware of our inner experience and learning to befriend what is going on inside ourselves." Another way to interpret this is to say that we need to become friends with all of the parts of who we are, and the best way to do that is to allow them to be heard. No excuses. No hiding. No judgment. Instead, pure love and support for this soul that lives inside of your body to express in the way that feels most right. If not for yourself, for others because, like I said, we need examples to show us that this way of living is not only possible, it is necessary. What a gift you have inside of you. Allow your body to speak and when it does, listen and trust what comes out and what comes next.

I want to get ahead of a thought that may be brewing inside of you. The work of becoming embodied, feeling empowered and living elevated requires a lot of self-reflection, self-compassion, and self-awareness. Self. Self. Self. There is often fear associated with being seen as selfish because we've been conditioned to prioritize others' needs and expectations above our own. Often society labels self-care and personal time as self-centered, leading to guilt or shame when we put ourselves first. I want to offer another perspective. **This type of work is not about neglecting others, nor is it being inconsiderate. It's about prioritizing the importance of living a life of truth.** When we do that, we not only feel happier, we empower others to do the same. So, really, being selfish is a selfless act. When we practice a healthy level of "selflessness," we are giving ourselves the opportunity to remember who we are and what we are meant to be in this world. We also become better equipped to support those we love. It's like the airplane safety instructions: Secure your oxygen mask before helping others because you can't assist if you're not okay yourself.

This commitment to self isn't always comfortable. Sometimes it means making choices that others might not understand or questioning traditions we've always accepted. The following story illustrates exactly what I mean about honoring your truth, even when it challenges expectations.

RECLAIMING MY NAME

A couple of years into my marriage, I started feeling uneasy about taking my husband's last name. I didn't realize what a big deal this was until people started calling me by a last name I was not born with. Every time I heard it, something felt off. I didn't like being identified in this way. I knew this because my head would heat up, and many times, my stomach felt like it was in knots.

For a while, I chose to ignore these signals. Then, as time went on, they got more intense and eventually could not be ignored. I started to journal to keep track of what I was feeling and how long the feelings would last. I thought that if I could track the patterns, it would allow me to make sense of what was going on. As I was doing this, I started to notice fear. I would ask myself, *What am I afraid of? Did I make the wrong choice? Was I not supposed to be in this marriage?* In order to calm myself down, I had to tell myself that the only action to take was to listen to my body, period. I did not need to make any big decisions; I just needed to allow myself to feel and sit with my feelings.

When I got married, taking his name felt like the obvious choice. It seemed like the natural step, especially since we were planning to start a family. What I didn't realize was how much taking his name would make me feel like I had given a part of myself away. For 30 years, I had been Jen Aks, and in an instant, that all changed. I didn't grow up in a culture where women were considered the property of their husbands or where taking their last name was a symbol of a transfer of ownership, but for whatever reason, the whole thing felt off to me. Maybe it was the indirect messages in our culture—narratives ingrained in fairytales, movies and books that we can't escape. Who really knows? I didn't. So, instead, I surrendered. I decided to trust whatever was coming. I knew that what I was experiencing was not regret about getting married or a lack of love for him; it was about the ease with which I let go of who I was.

The University of Iowa did a study showing that our bodies can detect and respond to stimuli even before our conscious minds are aware, known as "preconscious processing." This basically means that **our bodies reveal truths before our minds are ready to accept them.** In other words, the wisdom inside of us is able to perceive and react to what we cannot yet see or understand. Pretty wild, right? That is exactly what was happening to me. My body told me that something wasn't right, that a shift needed to take place, and so, I decided to listen.

After talking about it with him, we agreed on a hyphenated version. This definitely gave me some relief, however, I could not shake this unsettled feeling that I had still abandoned myself. From that point on, I made a promise that I would always listen to my body and trust that the nudges I was feeling were valid and needed to be expressed. This commitment did not come without fear because our body is where our truth lives, and our truth is sometimes hard to face, and wow, was I about to face the hardest truth of my life? I will share that story with you soon. For now, I will say that reclaiming my name, even partially, gave me enough alignment and a sense of re-embodiment to move forward in a way that felt right at the time. So I offer this to you: **When you hear a nudge, listen. You don't need to make some massive leap—just take one small step toward what feels true because each small step builds the trust you need to make the most aligned choices.**

IT'S OKAY TO CHANGE

Do you ever notice how people apologize for changing? I believe that changing how we feel, shifting our perspective, or deciding something different today than we would have yesterday is a sign that we are evolving, expanding, and becoming even more wise and incredible.

Take politics, for example. A leader might start as a Democrat and later identify as a Republican, or vice versa, and somehow, it's viewed as a betrayal rather than growth. Or a teacher might completely change their approach to education after discovering new research, moving from traditional methods to innovative practices. Or a parent might realize their strict parenting style isn't working for their child and choose to become more flexible and understanding. Why is that seen as a bad thing or a failure? For some reason, there's this unspoken expectation that once we've chosen a path or held a belief, we must stay locked into it forever. I've never understood that. Aren't we supposed to shift, reflect, and grow as we gain new information and insight?

Personally, I've found so much freedom in giving myself permission to shift. I believe that it is an essential part of becoming the empowered leader we are meant to be. Whether it's leading our children, our teams, or ourselves, strong leaders change, evolve, and adapt. I like to think of it like the seasons. Just as nature changes, so do we. The leaves turn, the air cools, and the landscape transforms. These shifts don't just happen; they're necessary. They bring opportunities for growth and renewal, so why would it be different for humans?

Each time we face something that scares us—each time we step outside of that comfort zone—we come face to face with aspects of ourselves we couldn't have known otherwise. That resistance you may feel when change comes knocking is where the magic is. That's where different aspects of ourselves speak, showing us exactly what needs healing and what beliefs are ready to be questioned. **When we lean into change instead of away from it, we create opportunities for self discovery that simply aren't possible when everything stays the same.**

The interesting thing is, not everyone sees it this way. People may react when they see us moving away from the version of ourselves they were comfortable with. They might fear that this inner power could challenge their own understanding of themselves. But that's their reaction, not your problem.

I truly believe that the more we allow ourselves to evolve, the more we come home to our truth, our power, and our purpose. But how do we navigate this evolution when we hold such complex feelings about change? This is where **the YES, AND mindset** comes into play.

THE YES/AND MINDSET

While bodyset is a primary focus for The Power of Gesture, mindset is absolutely part of the equation. The YES/AND mindset amplifies our ability to change because it removes the pressure to choose just one way:

- YES, I can honor a love that brought me joy AND recognize when it's time for a change.
- YES, I will be grateful for the lessons I learned from my parents AND allow myself the freedom to find a new path.
- YES, I am excited about a new opportunity AND feel deep sadness about leaving the comfort of where I am now.
- YES, I am proud of setting a boundary with my friend AND feel guilt for the distance it's creating in the relationship.

The YES/AND mindset gives us permission to hold multiple truths at the same time. So, give yourself permission to embrace the freedom of change because guess what? You don't have to choose. How empowering is that!

If you would like to explore your YES/AND statements, please visit www.jenaks.com/yourbodyisspeaking

SURRENDER'S POWER

We've explored giving ourselves permission, living our unapologetic truth, reclaiming our identity, embracing change, and adopting the YES, AND mindset. Each of these has been about actively choosing and claiming our power. Now, there's a final and essential step in this journey—one that may seem counterintuitive after all this talk of empowerment: the ability to surrender.

Unlike permission which we consciously grant ourselves, surrender asks us to let go and allow the guidance from within to lead the way. Where permission is actively claiming your power, surrender is trusting the power that's already there.

Many think of surrender as waving the white flag—an admission of defeat, weakness, or failure. We've been conditioned to believe that surrendering means giving up, abandoning our power, or submitting to something against our will. But this misunderstanding has kept so many of us trapped in cycles of struggle—fighting to control outcomes, resisting what we feel, and gripping tightly to plans that no longer serve us. I believe that surrender is one of the most empowering acts we can do for ourselves because when we surrender, we're not giving away our power—we're reclaiming it. True surrender allows us to remain curious students of life, open to becoming all the versions of ourselves we're meant to be.

Don't get me wrong, surrender doesn't mean we stop taking action—instead, it means that our actions come from a place of truth rather than fear. When you surrender to the wisdom within, you don't become less—you become more. More present. More powerful. More authentic. More alive. You're being honest and allowing deeper information to nourish your soul.

LET'S SUMMARIZE WHAT WE KNOW

1. **Self-Reflection and Awareness:** Taking time to self-reflect on our values, what we believe in, and interests we care about is an important step in breaking free from old patterns or conditioning that we may be holding on to.

2. **Authenticity's Ripple Effect:** When we give ourselves permission to be authentic and show up unapologetically, we are giving others permission to do the same. What a gift!

3. **Feel It to Create It:** Neville Goddard teaches us to "assume the feelings of the wish fulfilled." When we embody our desired future feelings right now, our nervous system can't tell the difference between imagination and reality. This is how we make our desired shifts—by feeling our way into our future.

Releasing What Was, Embracing What Is

The Power of Gesture: **Releasing What Was, Embracing What Is** will give you an opportunity to embody and feel the concept of surrender by releasing and breaking free from what no longer serves you. I'm going to modify it here; however, you can experience a longer version by scanning the QR code at the end of this chapter or by visiting www.jenaks.com/yourbodyisspeaking, where you will find The Power of Gesture chapter videos. Press play, and I will be there to guide you through the experience.

STEP 1: INTENTION

Find a comfortable spot and take a moment to bodyset. Silently or aloud, declare your intention by saying: "I am able to release old patterns and align with my truth now."

STEP 2: IDENTIFY

Quietly ask yourself, "What expectations or rules am I ready to break free from?" It might be something tangible, like a story you've been told and lived by that no longer serves you. Or, it might be something more abstract, like a feeling of limitation or a pattern of thinking that holds you back. Having the expectation to be perfect has made me feel exhausted and never good enough. Being taught that asking for help makes me look weak has made me feel overwhelmed. Saying yes because I was told to agree with people older than me has made me feel disconnected from myself and my truth.

1. Name your the expectation.
2. Notice how it makes you feel.
3. Notice where you feel it in your body.

STEP 3: GESTURE #1: EMBODY

Use the information you just gathered to help you create your first gesture. Notice the quality of the emotion—is it restricting? Allow your hands to move in a way that connects to that feeling. Some examples could be exhaustion, so your shoulders get heavy. Overwhelm could be felt in the jaw, so our hands hold our jaw with some pressure. Or possibly, disconnection is felt in the throat, and the hands embody a gesture representing a closing off.

STEP 4: IDENTIFY

Now, see yourself releasing fully. Letting go.
1. Name the emotion. (Love, acceptance, relief?)
2. Notice how it makes you feel. (Peaceful, stronger?)
3. Notice where you feel it in your body.

STEP 5: GESTURE #2: EMBODY

Use the above information to create your second gesture—this could be an open and expansive gesture, a gesture of letting go.

STEP 6: INTEGRATE

Now we integrate both gestures by moving back and forth from the restriction to the relief a couple of times, allowing both parts to be acknowledged and heard.

TIPS FOR GESTURE PRACTICE

- **Bodyset:** Place one hand on your heart, one hand on your belly, and close your eyes.
- **Move slowly:** Allow yourself to express and listen to what your body is saying.
- **Repeat:** Repetition gives the body more time to process and communicate.
- **Music:** Choose a piece of music that inspires you.

STEP 7: JOURNAL .

I invite you to document how your body feels after the practice and reflect on any new realizations that may have been made.

> **Empowered Affirmation:** *"With each movement, I dissolve the boundaries of who I was told to be and embody the truth of who I am becoming."*

Ready to dive deeper? This QR code will take you to The Power of Gesture: Releasing What Was, Embracing What Is video, where you'll join me for a full immersive experience that brings these concepts to life.

CHAPTER 4

HEALING AND INTEGRATING

You have what you need within you to heal and empower your soul. It all starts with courage, willingness, and belief. Courage to face your fears, a willingness to try something new and to believe that empowered transformation is around the corner.

IN THIS CHAPTER, we're diving even deeper into what it means to truly empower ourselves—our past, our present, and our future. It's never too late to create the life you want, whether that's landing the job you've always dreamed of, finally teaching that course you've been developing for years, opening yourself to a new kind of love, moving to that city that keeps calling you, or writing the book that's been living in your body, waiting to be born.

My invitation is to draw wisdom from all your lived experiences—the beautiful moments, the challenging ones, and the lessons still unfolding—and map out the path toward where you want to go.

Inspired by Richard Schwartz's Internal Family Systems (IFS) work and Louise Hay's inner child and mirror practices, I've created accessible ways to explore the voices and lessons from our past, present, and future selves. My hope is that these practices will help you understand who you are at the deepest level and guide you toward who you're becoming.

I use the word *re-parent* in this chapter intentionally because, as children, our bodies and minds absorb everything around us—the words, the gestures, the unspoken and spoken rules that shape our understanding of who we are and how we move through the world. When we were young, we didn't have the tools to process these experiences, and we had no idea how they would live in our bodies. They simply became a part of us. But now we carry profound wisdom in our cells, born from every challenge we've faced and every triumph we've celebrated. This means we are no longer at the mercy of having to do something because we are told, or follow an old narrative that no longer serves us. We get to choose differently now.

Through some of the tools I teach in this chapter, you will see that you have the ability to extract the lessons from the past, integrate them into the present, and feel empowered because of it. **I invite you to view your life as an ongoing journey of self-discovery, where each reflection is an opportunity to heal old wounds, reclaim your inner strength, and create the life you truly desire.**

A visual that I love to use is a camera lens. Imagine seeing your life through a lens where you have the power to widen the frame, allowing more of your life to come into view. As it opens, your past slowly reveals itself and expands into your present. They blend, creating a beautiful representation of who you are. In this visualization, you invite all of your experiences and emotions in, allowing yourself to get reacquainted with open arms, deep compassion, and a desire to learn. You suddenly realize that everything you have experienced has happened for you, not to you, shifting struggle and pain into wisdom and transformation.

The story I am about to share is an experience that, at first glance, seemed like any ordinary moment. However, it quickly became clear that what was unfolding before me was something far deeper—a moment that would heal old wounds from my childhood and guide me toward my purpose.

There was no logical conversation happening; instead, I had a feeling, an undeniable sense, that this was a path worth exploring. I was drawn in, not just by what I saw but by what I felt. Had I known that what was in front of me would re-parent and heal my childhood wound, I may not have leaned in because of the weight and fear of the lesson. Not knowing allowed me to feel free, not overthink, and remain open to what led me in a direction my life was absolutely meant to go.

Life gives us these moments constantly—invitations that hold lessons waiting to be revealed. I invite you to listen to what's calling you, to trust what feels true, and to remain open to the possibility that what's in front of you might be exactly what your soul needs. I will share one of those moments from my life with you now.

RE-PARENTING MYSELF

My jaw dropped, mouth wide open, frozen with admiration. I was sitting in an auditorium at PS120, a New York City public elementary school, in awe. I felt love so big in my heart and a strong personal connection that was unclear at first. Before I could put words to what I was experiencing, I started to cry at the sight of 30 children embodying academic learning with movement.

National Dance Institute, founded by Jacques D'Amboise in 1976, is an organization that empowers approximately 6,500 NYC public school children a year through the arts. These kids were experiencing the very thing that I had longed for in my childhood. They were learning a curriculum with their body. They were being taught about the world through music, dance, and poetry. The teachers taught in a cadence with their voices that felt like a song while the children received and integrated the information while moving. Joyful rigor, high expectations, and, perhaps most importantly, they were taught with a set of specific techniques designed to ensure that every single child in the room was seen and valued no matter what.

You could feel the commitment to inclusivity as the children were being seen for who they were and validated for how they learned. My body was overwhelmed. It was as if I had discovered the answer to a question I had been searching for decades. This kinetic approach not only educated but empowered these young learners to stand taller, be brave, and step into the truth of who they were. As I watched, my body communicated an overwhelming "yes" to this work, and so I began what would become close to two decades of service to the next generation. As I did this, **I gained a level of personal mastery that not only allowed me to empower others but also to heal myself at the same time.**

I invite you to close your eyes and imagine classes of 30–50 that make up thousands of children on stages, in cafeterias, and in classrooms throughout the city, the country, and the world, learning a movement methodology that transforms lives and the way we learn. Picture children of all colors, races, languages, sizes, ages, and movement abilities coming together in a safe, brave space that celebrates the very core of who they are. Allow me to introduce you to one now.

I will never forget Sophia. I was teaching fifth grade at PS2 in Chinatown. I was using one of the brilliant techniques where we shift the architecture of the room so that every child is seen, so that no child can hide and, instead, can be celebrated for who they are. I split the group in half, parted them like the Red Sea, teaching from the center so that the children in the middle were now in the front, and there she was. This beautiful child, with a smile so bright, trying her best while struggling to get it right. Sophia had Down Syndrome, which didn't allow her to move as quickly as the other children. I saw her struggle, eyes down, staring at her feet, trying hard to work through it. She looked up, our eyes met, and my heart melted. It was as if our souls spoke, and I knew. In that moment, I made a commitment that her disability would not hold her back and that we would find unique ways for her to soar into her personal success.

As the year progressed, I continued to meet her where she was at and celebrate her strengths along the way. By the end of the year, she showed tremendous progress, so I invited her to join the NDI DREAM Project (Dancers Realize Excellence Through Arts and Movement), a scholarship program that provides children with and without disabilities the opportunity to perform. Sophia accepted and stayed with this program for years. From what I saw and what she expressed to me, those years transformed her life.

I've chosen to live in a world where believing in one another, celebrating individuality, and honoring self-expression are at the core of who we are. A world where each of us, regardless of age, background, or learning style, has something valuable to contribute, teach, and share. It's a world liberated from the constraints of "should be," embracing the expansive possibilities of "what is." It's a world I wish I had grown up in, one that might have spared me from the debilitating self-doubt that affected so many years of my life because I questioned who I was.

Now, it has become my mission to teach, to empower, and to celebrate our differences, preventing the seed of doubt from taking root like it did in me. I believe we can do that through the healing and integration practices we will explore here together.

As much as I stand as a teacher, I remain a lifelong student, learning from every unique soul I encounter. I am also the child who still needs to be re-parented, healed, and acknowledged for the experiences I had while growing up. To know that they served me, led me, and taught me the lessons I needed in order to do my work now. It was through my own struggles with doubt and lack of self-worth that I learned to truly see people for who they are—to see individuals like Sophia—and to see myself reflected in them. I now understand that the pain and struggles I've experienced have led me to this moment, sharing this book with you and empowering you to look back on your life, to learn, and then step forward to grow with the lessons revealed. This is where empowerment becomes more than a state of being; it becomes a way of living. To be the teacher and the student forever.

After mastering this incredible methodology, I knew that my impact would be greater if I taught those who were teaching others. I started training the teachers in NYC, and then I was sent to affiliates around the country. What I didn't realize was the impact this work would have on me. Two decades of embodying the very thing that I needed when I was a child was the exact medicine I needed to heal and re-parent my soul. This transformational journey was the bridge to bring me home to myself, to my success, to my body, and to my purpose. **It was being a part of National Dance Institute that allowed me to piece together the narrative of my life that was missing and realize that every step I had taken—every conversation I left because of feeling unworthy, every insecurity that weighed me down into darkness—had meaning and would be the very thing that would contribute to something greater.** I saw myself in these children. I saw the child that was hiding, unsure of their worthiness, and I was called to say, "I see you, I am going to meet you where you are and help you rise into your unique excellence." It was during these years that I came to understand that my story mattered because it could give voice to others and empower them to be who they are meant to be. Through this work, I not only found validation for my own story and was able to heal wounds that needed attention, but I also discovered a newfound sense of empowerment and strength in my voice. I was ready to take the leap and challenge myself in ways I never thought possible.

RE-PARENTING YOUR PARTS

Dr. Richard Schwartz, the Founder of Internal Family Systems (IFS) and author of *No Bad Parts*, teaches us that we have multiple "parts" or sub-personalities within us, each with its own beliefs, emotions, and perspectives based on its life experience. He teaches us that these parts hold valuable wisdom. Rather than fixing them, we approach them with curiosity and compassion to understand their roots and integrate them into a balanced Internal Family System. IFS is a process of reshaping our sense of self. Rather than being defined by any single experience or emotion, we realize that our identity is layered and composed of many "parts." Here's why I see that as extraordinary and beautiful. It helps us see that whatever emotion we are experiencing—be it anger, doubt, insecurity, fear, etc.—is just part of who we are, not all of who we are. These are temporary states that will eventually pass. This awareness invites our strong, capable, joyful, compassionate, and empathetic parts to chime in at any time to support the parts that are struggling. **This fuller understanding of self brings a fresh perspective that is both liberating and exciting because it allows us to see ourselves through a new lens—one that is compassionate rather than critical, curious rather than judgmental, and empowering rather than limiting. Instead of being defined by our struggles, we realize we're complex beings with many resources within us available to help us navigate whatever shows up.**

The other day, I led a workshop where one of the participants identified a part of her personality as whimsical, funny, and light-hearted. She embodied this energy with a playful gesture, moving her hands and arms as if scattering sparkles were all around her—it was absolutely beautiful. Later in the session, she uncovered another part of herself that often holds back the whimsical side—a heavy, burdened part that feels trapped by the weight of the world. She embodied this heavy energy by raising her hands above her head, palms facing up, as if trying to hold back an invisible force pushing her down, making her feel smaller and smaller, as though she was being buried under the ground. Heavy, right?

I immediately said, "Let's bring in the whimsical part to help the weighted part out." So, after she embodied the weight of the world with her burdened gesture, she immediately transmuted that energy with her hands by embodying the lighthearted, whimsical energy. After repeating the two gestures several times, allowing them to move back and forth between each other, with music, her energy completely shifted. She felt so much lighter and freer in her body, and she couldn't help but start to cry. She said, "Can it be this easy? I wonder if all of my other limiting beliefs have opposing thoughts that can come in and help." I told her that was 100 percent possible. I offered a thought that her whimsical part could be the one that comes to save the day for everyone. I said, "Why not allow your whimsical part to be your superhero where she visits all of your heavier, sad, doubtful, insecure parts and gives them a little love as well?" Watching her embody this realization was profound because it's a truth we can all take with us. There is so much power in recognizing that we don't have to let any one part define us or weigh us down. We can lean on our strengths and let them work in harmony to lighten the load and help us move forward.

Integrating our parts instead of resisting them—that's where the magic happens. When we stop fighting what's inside us, those parts actually begin to soften and transform on their own. What if we asked instead of told? Got curious instead of judged? You might think, "Sure, sounds great in theory, but who can actually do this?" Trust me, I've been there. I've watched this work—both in my own journey and with those I've guided. It's not about getting it right every time. It's about having the courage to face what may be uncomfortable and believe transformation is possible. One of the most common needs among all humans is the desire to be seen and validated. I love this quote from Oprah Winfrey. She said: "I've talked to nearly 30,000 people on this show, and all 30,000 had one thing in common—they all wanted validation. They all wanted to be heard, and they all wanted to know that what they said mattered." When looking at our internal world in the way I just framed it, why wouldn't Oprah's words apply to the "parts" inside of us? We can make a choice to treat those parts with the same respect we would offer another person. **Choice is important because it is something we can control. We can choose to become curious about ourselves with the intention to learn.** The truth is that much of our fear, doubt, and shame stems from our childhood, where we didn't have the awareness to choose. We had an experience, and these parts got stuck because we didn't know how to listen and process. We now have a choice to lean in, and give ourselves the respect we deserve by getting to know all of who we are.

Dr. Richard Schwartz highlights that within our parts, there is a leader, and that leader is your Self (with a capital S). He describes the Self as the "core essence of a person" who is wise and capable of healing and serves as the compassionate leader for the internal community that is within you. Self is always there, ready to support, much like a parent with unconditional love. Self is the highest version of you—untouched, unaffected, and unafraid—and the more we lean into our other parts with curiosity and compassion, the more activated Self becomes. To know that you have this resource within you to help guide and navigate your life is exciting. Let's have fun with this by empowering the Self inside of you with a visualization exercise. Allow me to set the stage.

GIVE EACH PART THE MIC

Imagine a stage inside your body. This is *your* imagined stage, so it can be as elaborate or as simple as you would like. My imagination tends to run wild, so for me, my stage is an oval shape with a bohemian rug and two cozy chairs with fluffy pillows facing the audience. One chair is for Self, and one is for an emotion. The emotion that comes to the stage is there to express what they couldn't when they first came into your life, most likely during childhood. These emotional parts of you have their own unique look, feel, and voice. Each is there to express who they are, where they came from, and why they feel the way they do. Often, these are the parts we push aside or abandon, thinking they don't need our attention. The truth is, they do, and this is their chance. I invite you to see these parts as little people within you, waiting to be acknowledged, nurtured, and loved.

Your inner leader, the Self, is on stage as the host, similar to a therapist, sitting in one of the chairs and listening with an open heart. The Self is grounded, confident, compassionate, and offers this safe space for these emotions to express and feel understood.

This exercise is not just about allowing your parts to vent, scream, cry, and share their stories; it's a creative way to see yourself through a new lens and to know that every emotion has something valuable to share and teach. It also reminds us that we are made of many "parts", not just one. I have found this perspective so helpful in lowering the volume on limiting beliefs and raising the volume on self-worth and confidence. **Giving ourselves the opportunity to hear the question "What do you need?" and answer honestly is sometimes all we need to heal some of our deepest wounds.** I've written out six clear steps to follow so that you can begin to set the stage for your emotions to grab the mic. Read through the steps, sit in a quiet place, and allow yourself to surrender to what is possible.

1. BODYSET

Find a place where you can sit quietly without distractions. Place one hand on your heart, one on your belly, and close your eyes.

2. USE YOUR IMAGINATION

Use your imagination to set the stage. Design a space that feels inviting, supportive, and welcoming. Allow your imagination to bring in color and textures. Notice if there are any shifts in your energy or facial expressions. Are you smiling? Curious? Excited?

3. INVITE EMOTIONS TO SPEAK

See your Self, the highest part of you, sitting in one of the chairs or cushions on the floor. Once you feel ready, invite an emotion up to stage so that they can share their story. For example: if the emotion is fear, you might say out loud or quietly to yourself, *"Fear, what do you want me to know? What do you need?"* Allow the emotion to take on a form; this could be a person, an object, or energy. Whatever it is, allow it to speak and remain open to what you hear.

4. FEEL THE ROLE OF SELF

As you listen to the emotion, feel the role of Self, a grounded, compassionate host there to support and learn.

5. GESTURE

At this point, you may feel a connection to the emotion. I invite you to embody that emotion with a hand gesture. That gesture could be having your hands out in front of you, palms to the ceiling, feeling the energy rest in the center of them. Or, you may feel called to show this emotion gratitude by placing both hands on your heart. However you choose to gesture toward this part of you, it is 100% right.

6. CLOSING

Afterward, take a few deep breaths and bring yourself back to the present moment. Reflect on the experience, consider journaling, and notice how your relationship toward this part has shifted.

This exercise is another reminder of the tools we have within ourselves to heal. How beautiful to celebrate your parts in this way. Instead of shaming them and making them feel bad with "I should" or "I wish I didn't feel" statements, you are welcoming all of you with love. How empowering! **Once we have created an environment within us where all parts can coexist with ease, we can see our life experiences a bit more clearly and open up to each experience as an invitation to grow.**

This approach allows us to understand why certain patterns continue to show up in our lives - and more importantly, why we sometimes stay in situations longer than we think we "should". It's often because there's still something to learn, something our parts are trying to teach us.

Have you ever felt that a relationship in your life lingered longer than it "should" have? You had a gut feeling that it was wrong, but you stayed anyway because, for whatever reason, you felt you didn't think you could leave. You may have been scared and ashamed, and even though you knew it wasn't right, you kept going back because you weren't done yet. The truth? You hadn't learned the lesson or lessons that relationship was meant to teach you, so you weren't done. You probably had people around you saying, "Why are you going back again? They treat you so badly; what is wrong with you?"

What if you knew better and were able to say, "I'm not done yet, I have not learned the lesson(s) I am supposed to and need to stay in this relationship until I do." Most likely, you didn't have that response because you didn't know there was a lesson to be learned, one that would serve this part of you in your future self. In this approach to re-parenting yourself, you can now accept this invitation to more deeply understand and grow from what you learn.

Life is constantly extending its hand to us, offering opportunities to grow, heal, and transform—teaching us to trust our gut when the pull toward something becomes stronger than the fear holding us back. In these kinds of moments, we face a choice: shrink back or trust and dive in. When we accept these invitations—especially the scary ones—incredible things happen. Trust becomes the bridge that restores our self-worth, reminding us what we're truly capable of. How many times have you surprised yourself by doing the very thing you thought you couldn't? And how many of those times have you stood there afterward thinking, "I can't believe I just did that?" I had that experience when I was invited to direct a show for National Dance Institute. The invitation terrified me, yet at the same time, it ignited a pull that was undeniable.

VOICES OF CHANGE

As I shared earlier, National Dance Institute's movement methodology healed so much of my soul. This was true, AND I didn't realize there was more to be done. An invitation showed up, one that created a surge of doubt, reminiscent of my younger years because I wasn't sure that I could achieve what seemed like an impossible task.

Each year, National Dance Institute selects a theme that serves as the curriculum to teach 6,500 public school children and influences the affiliates around the world. Of the 6,500 children in NYC, approximately 200 are chosen to fully manifest the theme and perform it on a professional stage with 12–15 choreographed pieces, a full orchestra, lighting, design, costumes, projections, and more. The annual theme comes from a vision created by a chosen director for that year. In 2019, that director was me.

"Voices of Change" was inspired by my deep fascination and admiration for the '70s. To me, this decade symbolized freedom, liberation, and possibility. It was a time led by individual expression through activism, politics, the arts, and fashion, where boundaries seemed almost non-existent. I always felt connected with this decade because it embodied everything I believe about trusting our body's wisdom. I loved how people expressed authenticity in every way— allowing their physical, emotional, and spiritual expression to lead a social revolution. It was the ultimate example of bodies speaking louder than words ever could.

My vision for this show was to expose the generation I was teaching to this incredible period in our history, with the intention to inspire their own individuality and explore the endless possibilities of how they can make their voices heard in the world. I taught them to realize that advocacy can transcend the conventional methods of speaking into a microphone to lead a protest march. They can also have their voices heard through vibrant, colorful, painted works of art on a canvas that conveys a powerful message, or they could write a poem about what they care about, join a drum circle that expresses unity, or wear an outfit that makes a statement that is meaningful to them.

My goal was to nourish their souls—to encourage their bodies to speak their truth through the integration of choreography, music, and visual art. By highlighting heroes like Malala Yousafzai, Nelson Mandela, Marianne Williamson, The Newsies, The Children of the Birmingham March, Harry Belafonte, and Aretha Franklin, "Voices of Change" unlocked hundreds of unique minds inspiring creativity, innovation, and hope for the next generation.

When I think back on that experience, I am in awe. I still cannot believe that I wrote and directed something so profound, something that required research around topics I grew up knowing nothing about. When I pause to ask myself how I could have accepted such an invitation, I think it's because I knew deep down that I was capable of doing it. Don't get me wrong, there were several moments during the creation of this show when my doubt took the mic and tried to hijack the flow, squash my vision, and hold me back from fully expressing my true self. In those moments, I would bodyset by getting quiet, closing my eyes, placing my hands on my body, and breathing into the intention of reconnecting to my power. I would remind myself that I was chosen to direct this show, and if I weren't capable, I would not be in that role.

One might think that after experiencing what felt like the peak of my life and the fullest expression of my true self, self-doubt would never return. But that's not the case. Doubt, like many of the emotions connected to our past experiences, lingers, often remaining stuck in the body. As Bessel van der Kolk teaches in *The Body Keeps the Score*, trauma is not just a memory in our minds but a physical imprint in our bodies. Similarly, Peter Levine's work in **Somatic Experiencing** emphasizes that healing requires us to reconnect with our bodies, allowing us to feel and release the stored tension and emotional pain.

This is why having a framework like Embody, Empower, Elevate is so important. During those 12 months, while developing the show, I repeatedly cycled through all three phases—knocked off course into doubt, then realigned with my voice, and stepped back into my power with greater clarity each time. The more I practiced this cycle, the quicker my recovery became and the bolder my choices grew. With time, the 3 E's will do the same for you, becoming a framework to fall back on when life inevitably pulls you off track.

YOUR YOUNGER SELF HOLDS THE ANSWERS

At 50 years old, I never expected to turn to a younger version of myself for guidance, and yet that's exactly what I needed. During a time of uncertainty, my life coach encouraged me to go within and peel back the layers of my experiences to uncover the answers I needed. This process led me to explore my inner child, a concept I had heard about before but had always dismissed because it didn't resonate.

With my coach's guidance, I accepted the invitation and dove in. Who knew that a Little Jen inside of me needed to be held, heard, validated, and most importantly, experience even deeper healing? I needed to help her feel secure, but before doing that, I needed to know why she was there in the first place. This journey of self-reflection became one of the most profound lessons of my life.

I was reminded of the stories she was holding on to and the emotional connection she had to them. There was one in particular when I was humiliated by the school principal in second grade. During an all-school assembly, I was called to the stage to stand in front of the entire student body because I was talking. I wasn't only asked to walk onstage, I was asked to turn around, have my back to the audience, put my nose against the curtain wall, and stand there for what felt like an eternity. The embarrassing energy rushed into my body and, unfortunately, found a home for many years to come. The home of shame. A home that, over the years, built a foundation that felt impossible to break.

I remembered this during a meditation when I allowed my inner Jen to speak. I woke up to parts of myself that had been buried for so long. As painful as it was to feel the humiliation of this memory, and the ones that built on top of it, I knew that in order to become fully alive with my empowered self, I had to feel it and let it out. I turned to the imagined stage in my head where my "Self" was waiting in the chair with open arms. The shame part of me came to the stage, vented, cried, and threw a bit of a tantrum. It was painful, but I felt safe. While feeling sad about this, I put my hand out, palm facing the sky, imagining that my shame was right in the middle of it, feeling held for the very first time. I then created a second gesture with my other hand, a circular motion that moved slowly, surrounding the hand holding the shame, giving it an energy of love.

As I cried, I felt like I was healing myself. By allowing the shame to speak and be heard, it naturally transformed from something heavy to something lighter. It was amazing! This is the essence of what this book is about: We have the power within us to heal and know what we need next. It is real. It is possible, and it is wildly empowering!

I invite you to bodyset for a moment. Close your eyes, place one hand on your heart, one hand on your belly, and picture your younger self. See them clearly. What color is their hair? What are they wearing? How old are they? You can call on a memory or a photo to help you reconnect. When you feel the energy of your younger self, simply say, "I see you, I get you, you are not alone." You will be amazed at how something so simple can shift your energy and open the door to a lighter, more compassionate feeling toward the memory.

As I've emphasized throughout this book, when experiences happen to us as children, we simply aren't equipped with the tools to process them properly, and as a result, they get stuck in our body. This is why van der Kolk's research on the body storing trauma is so crucial to our healing journey. I keep returning to this concept because it's fundamental to understanding why traditional "thinking our way out" approaches often fall short. **Our bodies hold these memories physiologically—not just as thoughts but as physical imprints requiring a somatic approach to release.** This principle underscores everything we've explored so far and is why I want to offer you yet another powerful way to transmute these feelings and thoughts when they get loud in your body.

MIRROR WORK

Mirror work, developed by Louise Hay, founder of Hay House, is a transformative self-love practice that empowers individuals to shift negative thoughts and emotions into positive, uplifting ones. The practice teaches us to look into our eyes, speak loving and affirming words to create shifts in our energy, and reconnect with our truth. This seems simple, and to a degree, it is; however, like anything else, what shows up can be profound and needs to be processed.

Recently, I was dancing in my living room to release emotion. I found myself moving toward the bathroom. As I entered, I caught my reflection in the mirror and became locked in what felt like a stare-off. It was as though I was staring into the depths of my soul, seeing myself in a way I never had before. The clarity with which I saw my own eyes and the energy behind them was both eerie and captivating. This experience led me to a personal variation of the mirror work I had learned about. Before I could verbalize an affirmation, I heard a whisper saying, "Trust yourself; it's going to be okay." I was taken aback. Tears slowly dripped down my face as I was going through a major shift in my life at that time.

Hearing those words was affirming and comforting. Then, I heard more. "I'm sorry for abandoning you. I'm sorry for ever doubting your intelligence. I'm sorry for allowing childhood doubts to linger for so long. I'm sorry for the pain I caused by allowing society to define you before you had the tools to do it yourself."

WOW… I was overwhelmed because this was unexpected. This experience made me realize that even with the tools we learn we can also create a unique version where our body speaks first and leads the way. With that said, I want to offer you a few affirmations, some of which Louise Hay used often. You can use these to jumpstart the mirror work, play with being prepared in front of the mirror, and then after a while, allow your body to lead:

1. "I deeply love and approve of myself just as I am."
2. "I forgive myself and set myself free."
3. "I am safe, and all is well in my world."

Pick one affirmation that resonates with you. Then approach the mirror with curiosity rather than expectation. As you look into your own eyes, allow a moment of pure presence before doing anything else. You might use the affirmation you chose, or a voice within may speak before you've even begun your affirmation—if so, simply listen. You might feel moved to gesture toward your reflection with your hands, creating another layer of connection. There's no wrong way to do this work. The beauty lies in experimenting and discovering the approach that creates the deepest shift for you.

What surprised me most about my own mirror practice was how naturally it evolved from affirmation into forgiveness. When I realized this was the medicine my soul needed, I took it one step further by writing myself a forgiveness letter. I'm sharing mine here as a model, in case this approach resonates with you:

"I realize I let society's view of intelligence shape how I saw you, which caused pain for so many years. I now recognize that, at the time, I didn't have the awareness or tools to see it differently. I am sorry for allowing those beliefs to define you and define us for so long, and I'm grateful for the lessons that came from it. Thank you for hearing this. I need you to know how sorry I am."

The moment I completed this letter and read it to myself in the mirror, I immediately heard a voice inside of me say: "You are smart. You are capable. You are uniquely talented. You are whole." I embodied this energy with my arms wide open, then moved into an enormous self-hug. I felt like I had 20 therapy sessions all in one. The whole thing felt like a purification for my soul, and as the tears flowed, I felt a surge of strength, a resilience born from facing my truth. It was honestly one of the greatest experiences of my life. What a catharsis!

When we forgive, we let go, and that release opens us up to so many possibilities—possibilities of love, connection, and a freedom that can make you feel like you can do anything. You have what you need within you to heal and empower your soul. It starts with courage, willingness, and belief. Courage to face your fears, a willingness to try something new, and to believe that empowered transformation is around the corner. I share my stories and the stories of others to show you that it is possible.

Have you ever experienced that moment when you hear words spoken or read them somewhere and they are the exact right message you need to hear in that moment? That feeling when you read something and it's like the universe is speaking directly to you? Years ago, I came across a passage that literally stopped me in my tracks. As I read each line, I felt layers of self-doubt and limitation peeling away. The words resonated so deeply that they became a turning point in my journey. I've returned to them countless times since, and each reading reveals something new. I want to share these powerful words with you now:

Our deepest fear is not that we are inadequate. Our deepest fear is that we are powerful beyond measure. It is our light, not our darkness that most frightens us. We ask ourselves, "Who am I to be brilliant, gorgeous, talented, fabulous?" Actually, who are you not to be? You are a child of God. Your playing small does not serve the world. There is nothing enlightened about shrinking so that other people won't feel insecure around you. We are all meant to shine, as children do. We were born to manifest the glory of God that is within us. It's not just in some of us; it's in everyone. And as we let our own light shine, we unconsciously give other people permission to do the same. As we are liberated from our own fear, our presence automatically liberates others.

—Marianne Williamson

When we truly absorb Marianne's words, we can recognize a profound truth: often, what blocks our light isn't external circumstances but our own limiting beliefs. We dim our brightness because somewhere along the way, we learned it was safer to be small. But what if there was a simple, practical way to begin reversing this pattern? What if you could literally "flip the switch" on the thoughts that keep you playing small?

This is where awareness meets transformation—understanding that we may fear our own power. So, how do we overcome that? I have a tool that I am so incredibly excited to share with you. It's simple, AND it works. It's a practice I've used many times when I find myself shrinking back from my own light, feeling intimidated by a situation I need to take care of, or questioning myself about anything. It's a powerful and accessible way to flip your thoughts and emotions into something that will serve you and keep you moving forward.

THE FLIP THE SWITCH METHOD

The last three years of my life have been a bit of a whirlwind filled with tough choices, emotional rollercoasters, and massive transitions. Not too long ago, I found myself stuck in a limiting mindset where my guilt and grief were weighing me down and having me second-guess a major decision that I had made. The one thing I knew I could do to feel better was to bodyset so I sat quietly on my meditation pillow with my legs crossed, eyes closed with a hand gesture out in front of me. I asked, *"How do I release guilt and grief and stop apologizing for what I knew was the right choice."*

I immediately heard, *"Transcend your guilt and grief into faith and love."* I was blown away! I felt this rush of aliveness move through my hands and into my body, which put me into an aligned state where everything felt right. I proceeded by saying out loud, "I am transcending my guilt and grief into faith and love." I repeated it, again and again. Then, I added a gesture of love by placing my hands on my heart, and in no time at all, my body and mind were aligned and experiencing gratitude. My energy and focus shifted by flipping the switch, shifting the words, and allowing this new thought to become the embodied affirmation that put me back into alignment with my power. Here are some examples of how you can flip the switch in your everyday life experiences.

"I've ruined my diet, I might as well give up completely."

Flip the switch: "I had a slip, I can make my next choice a healthy one."

"I had a bad day at work, I bet they are going to fire me."

Flip the switch: "Today was challenging, but tomorrow is a new day."

"I always pick the wrong people. I'll never have healthy relationships."

Flip the switch: "I'm learning what doesn't work for me, and getting clear on what I truly deserve."

"I'm so sorry, I don't know why I am crying, I'm probably being too sensitive."

Flip the switch: "I'm allowing myself to feel my emotions because they matter and deserve space."

"Other people have it worse, I don't know why I am complaining."

Flip the switch: "My feelings are valid, and honoring them helps me take better care of myself."

Now, there is one more step to the Flip the Switch Method: Create two hand gestures, one for the discomfort, fear, or worry and one for the empowering thought. Let's use the "I've ruined my diet; I might as well give up completely" as an example. This sentiment may be embodied by having your face lay in the palms of your hands, feeling defeated or another emotion. Then, create a gesture to match how you want to feel. "I had a slip, I can make my next choice a healthy one." This new empowering thought may have you move your hands from your face up to the sky that allows you to feel more open, forgiving, and strong. When doing the Flip the Switch Method, be sure to repeat and move slowly between both gestures several times to give yourself the time needed to realign. I have created a Flip the Switch worksheet for you to experiment with www.jenaks.com/yourbodyisspeaking

LET'S SUMMARIZE WHAT WE KNOW

1. **We're Not Just One Thing:** You have many parts within you—the confident one, the scared one, the playful one. These aren't flaws to fix but pieces that make you whole. When we embrace all of them instead of trying to be just one thing, that's when healing and liberation begin.
2. **Re-parenting Transforms:** Re-parenting doesn't require reliving the past, instead, it invites curiosity and compassion to soften old energy, making room for positive change.
3. **Your True Self is Whole**: Beneath all the layers of you is a steady, pure essence that remembers your truth.

Healing Through Integration

Now we're going to use The Power of Gesture to **Flip the Switch**. This experience can focus on either a childhood story you've been carrying or something more recent from your adult life.

I have modified it here; however, you can experience a longer version by scanning the QR code at the end of this chapter or by visiting www.jenaks.com/yourbodyisspeaking, where you will find The Power of Gesture chapter videos. Press play, and I will be there to guide you through the experience.

STEP 1: INTENTION

Find a comfortable position and bodyset. Place one hand on your heart, one hand on your belly, and take a deep breath. I invite you to state the intention quietly in your mind or out loud: "I acknowledge all parts of myself with love."

STEP 2: IDENTIFY

Think about a time when you recently asked yourself, "Why do I feel this way?" "How do I get rid of this feeling?" Maybe your thoughts sound something like: "I wish I wasn't so sad." "I wish I didn't doubt myself so much." "I want to have more confidence like her."

- Name the thought.
- Notice how it makes you feel.
- Notice where you feel it in your body.

STEP 3: GESTURE #1: EMBODY

Use the information you just gathered to help you create your first gesture. Notice the quality of the emotion and allow your hands to move in a way that connects to that feeling. For example, if you're feeling overwhelmed, your hands might press against your temples or create circular motions near your chest, as if stirring something chaotic inside. If you're experiencing sadness, maybe your hands draw inward toward your heart in a gentle gathering motion, collecting something special that feels scattered. Trust whatever hand gesture shows up.

STEP 4: IDENTIFY

Now, while you're experiencing Gesture #1, pause, and create a flip the switch statement.

Here are some examples:
Original thought: "Why do I feel this way?"
Flip the Switch: "My feelings matter and deserve space."

Original thought: "I want to have more confidence like her."
Flip the Switch: "I accept myself for all that I am."

Original thought: "How do I get rid of this feeling?"
Flip the Switch: "I can handle whatever comes my way."

STEP 5: GESTURE #2: EMBODY

Start with your original gesture, then connect to the energy of your flip-the-switch statement. Let that new feeling guide your hands into gesture #2—allow your body to show you what this empowering truth feels like.

STEP 6: INTEGRATE

Now it's time to integrate both gestures, flowing between the restriction and the relief. Move back and forth slowly a few times, letting both states coexist. This isn't about getting rid of one feeling—it's about honoring the full experience and allowing that natural duality to just be.

TIPS FOR GESTURE PRACTICE

- **Bodyset:** Place one hand on your heart, one hand on your belly, and close your eyes.
- **Move slowly**: Allow yourself to express and listen to what your body is saying.
- **Repeat:** Repetition gives the body more time to process and communicate.
- **Music:** Choose a piece of music that inspires you.

STEP 7: JOURNAL

I invite you to document how your body feels after the practice and reflect on any new realizations that may have been made.

> **Empowered affirmation:** *I flow through each phase— Embody, Empower, and Elevate—trusting the process, realigning with ease, and rising stronger every time.*

Ready to dive deeper? This QR code will take you to The Power of Gesture: Healing Through Integration video, where you'll join me for a full immersive experience that brings these concepts to life.

PART THREE
ELEVATE

CONGRATULATIONS! You have become embodied and are ready to take inspired action towards living an elevated life. The elevated phase is about fulfillment and service—a deep sense of contentment that arises from within, no longer tied to external validation. Elevate is where service becomes the natural, outward expression of this inner wholeness.

Let's focus on the fulfillment aspect for a moment. Living elevated is truly a time when you have arrived to know what matters most. Your voice. Your feelings. Your thoughts. Your desires. All of you! Living elevated can feel like relief because it means you are comfortable in your skin and are able to enjoy the simple pleasures in life, like sitting with a cup of coffee in the morning, smiling because you are content, not allowing the outside pressures of life to affect you. You care less about what other people think. You don't take others' advice to heart the way you used to. You have slowed down enough to listen to your body and you trust what it says. This is where deep joy takes place because you not only see the world differently, you are also able to incorporate your life's lessons in empowered and aligned ways. You see what is around you and live in the wonder of continued growth. It is such an honor to be taking you through this next phase because I know how it is going to positively impact your life!

I am going to start by going into more depth about what it means to elevate, why it matters, and what becomes possible when doing so. But first, let's review.

At the beginning of this book, we uncovered the root of your disconnection, the places where you may have lost sight of your truth, possibly without even realizing it. The good news is that you have gained perspective on what may have created that disconnection. My hope is that you've learned from that awareness and have forgiven how you got there. At this point, you have experienced The Power of Gesture enough times where you can incorporate it into your life continuing on the path of breaking free from conformity, listening deeply to your truth, and healing from patterns that no longer serve you. Through the process of re-parenting yourself and feeling empowered by this deeper understanding, you are ready. Ready to live in this elevated state—where claiming who you are, and living fully expressed doesn't seem like a distant dream, rather it's a reality that is waiting for you to claim.

WHAT IS IT?

Living elevated is when you've committed to yourself that you will honor your truth and make decisions that are aligned with your highest self, filled with intention, presence, and purpose. Here's the thing. We know that nothing is stagnant, so while we live elevated, we also accept and understand that moving between the 3 E's is part of the journey. When life throws a curveball and suddenly we're back needing to become embodied again, we don't panic. Instead, we embrace this reality. We recognize this is part of the journey, not a setback. And, we stand in gratitude—grateful that we now have the tools to help us bodyset, reset, and begin again. There's a profound appreciation that comes from this presence because we know that every moment we are taken off track is an opportunity to realign.

WHY DOES IT MATTER?

This is where the second part of living elevated comes into play. **When we live elevated, we not only have the ability to be present, we are now able to go beyond ourselves into the service of others. It's no longer just about personal growth; it's about collective elevation.** This is where we naturally discover that true fulfillment comes through service, not as a sacrifice, but as a result of our own work in reaching a state of wholeness.

It's so exciting because when we elevate it becomes a ripple that touches everyone around us, permitting others to claim their truth, and; set boundaries that honor themselves. Service isn't something you "should" do once you're elevated—it's what happens organically when you're no longer depleting yourself to please others or prove your worth. You serve from abundance rather than lack, from clarity rather than obligation. This is why elevation matters beyond personal transformation—because a world of embodied, empowered individuals naturally creates communities that thrive through mutual care rather than competition and exploitation. Do you feel it?

HOW WILL IT IMPROVE YOUR LIFE?

Living elevated allows you to speak your truth and know that what you have to say matters. You know how to listen to your body and trust its guidance. This understanding provides a sense of ease in your decisions and a confidence to allow the ebbs and flows of life. There is a calm, an ability to surrender to how life unfolds without being attached to an outcome. How liberating! Lastly, self-trust expands even further because you believe that what shows up is meaningful, and you have the wisdom to be curious and allow it to serve you rather than push it away.

Living elevated allows you to see the world in a way that you couldn't before, and that is because you did the work to clear your body from energy that no longer serves you. **You are not only ready to fly, you are willing to accept that you are forever a student on a continued path of learning about who you are and what is possible.**

One of my favorite things about the elevated phase is that, because it's a phase of true authentic alignment, we are able to receive the quiet lessons that life has to offer. I call them our unexpected teachers. We will explore some of them in Chapter 5.

CHAPTER 5

COURAGEOUS EXPRESSION: LIVING FROM THE INSIDE OUT

The path of coming home to ourselves isn't a destination but instead a practice—one that requires courage, patience, and compassion.

YOU MADE IT! You are here—elevated in your awareness, in your ability to speak up about the things you care about, in your approach to the world with how you move through it, and in your leadership. You are ready for this next phase of your journey.

Please know this: No matter where you find yourself right now—whether you're feeling fully transformed or still navigating challenges—simply engaging with these practices and reaching this chapter represents significant growth. Progress isn't always a straight line, and transformation happens in its own perfect timing. Some parts of you may feel completely awakened while others still need gentle attention, and that's exactly as it should be. With that said, you have begun awakening parts of yourself that allow you to see what's in front of you, next to you, and in the distance with greater clarity.

You're developing a heightened awareness that allows you to connect with things in a deeper way, whether it's something tangible—like people and nature—or intangible, like energy. You are becoming more aware and ready to receive what is revealing itself, and to give back to the world all that you have discovered within yourself.

Here's where we get into something a bit more abstract, yet so powerful. An elevated person becomes a natural magnet, where people are drawn to their presence—wanting to talk to them, be around them, share their stories with them. This magnetism goes beyond just attracting others who want to connect. They also attract unexpected teachers—people and experiences that offer wisdom and guidance often without realizing they're teaching at all.

UNEXPECTED TEACHERS: NATURE

When we're open to seeing nature as a guide, moments become invitations to pause, reflect, and connect with what's happening inside of us. It's a silent gesture, speaking to us in ways that go way beyond words. For example, a calm lake might reflect a moment in our life of stillness and introspection, while a river flowing in one direction can represent progress and movement toward a goal. The crashing waves of the ocean might echo the intensity or chaos of transformation in your life, reminding you of your ability to be resilient and powerful. These can be very strong messages and can provide insight in a moment when you need it most, yet didn't know it.

I love witnessing how nature's intelligence mirrors the intelligence that moves through our relationships. Here's what I mean: The river instinctively knows how to flow around rocks and islands, never resting and only responding. It carries the same wisdom as your body, instinctively moving toward what feels right and pulling away from what doesn't. This intelligence is all innate. When we pay attention, we realize we have an incredible source of guidance within.

UNEXPECTED TEACHERS: CHILDREN

Relationships are incredible, unexpected teachers. From your elevated perspective, you are able to view those once "toxic" relationships as some of the greatest sources of wisdom because you now know they taught you—what you truly value and what you want more or less of in your life. Maybe that job you once dreaded clarified your desire to wake up inspired rather than simply wanting to earn a paycheck.

And what about your children? They are some of the greatest teachers of our lives. Often, society teaches us to talk to them in a specific tone; for example, saying: *"You'll understand when you're older. You're not ready yet. You're too young to understand."* Living in an elevated perspective, you see that they are the ones carrying the wisdom you need. What if their souls chose us? What if they came to us because they are meant to teach us some of the most important lessons we need in our lifetime?

When we start thinking about life this way, the lessons appear everywhere. It could be as simple as watching a child run through a park with joy, reminding us of how good that once felt and helping us recognize that it's a feeling we want to experience again. As a result, we might decide to reset our day, inviting in the energy of freedom to take us in a new direction. Or perhaps, noticing someone struggling to cross the street reminds us that not everyone shares the same abilities. So as a result, we slow down, reset, and appreciate ourselves and others in a new way.

When we live elevated, we are able to live life with a higher consciousness and, as a result, see and feel things more deeply. So, take a moment. Look around and feel into the energies surrounding you: above, below, beside, and in front of you. This level of awareness is a gift. You will be amazed by the lessons you will learn and the shifts that will take place within you.

UNEXPECTED TEACHERS: RELATIONSHIPS

I had no idea that becoming a parent would be the education I needed most. The lessons I learned didn't come from parenting books or the well-intentioned advice of others; they came directly from my children. The fascinating part is that they had no idea they were teaching me. How could they? They were so young. It was their natural state of being, not even trying, that challenged me to open up and remember the truth of who I was.

At every stage of parenthood, even before a child is born, we're faced with decisions that will directly impact another human, and that is a huge responsibility. What foods will I eat to nourish the baby growing inside of me? What is the name that feels most right while balancing strong opinions from family? Then, the child arrives, and the questions just keep coming: What's the "right" way to feed my child, breast milk or formula, and for how long? What foods do I introduce? When do I allow someone else to hold them? Which vaccines do I give? Do I really need to sleep train them? And eventually, when is the right time to give them a phone? That last one might sound crazy, but it's real because we need to decide at what point we are handing our young kids over to a digital world that doesn't have their best interests at heart. I'll admit I struggled with this one big time, but eventually, I gave in.

From the moment my kids arrived, it felt like they were constantly holding up a mirror to my soul. Their innocent yet wise eyes would look into mine, and I felt like they were constantly asking, "Mom, who are you?" and "What do you truly believe?" It was as if they were reminding me that every decision I made was shaping their worldview, and that was not to be taken lightly. I really appreciated this challenge because it forced me to dig deep and awaken my soul in ways I never imagined. I found myself questioning, contemplating, and making sure that the decisions I made felt aligned with what was true for me and right for them.

Challenging societal norms for myself was one thing, but doing it for my children took on a whole different energy. My instincts spoke louder than ever before because these were two humans that I was raising, and my body refused to let outside influences dictate their path or label them before they could define themselves. The protective force in me was primal and fierce—exactly how our ancestors guarded their own. **I didn't always have the right answers, but I didn't need to. What I had was something far more reliable: my body telling me "this matters" with such clarity that I couldn't ignore it if I tried.**

In a world where social media constantly bombards us with picture-perfect family photos, stories of achievements, and idealized expressions of love, let's just say—kids or no kids—it's easy to get sucked into comparison. When I was raising my kids, it felt like every conversation with other parents circled around who was reading early or hitting developmental milestones on time. It was as if the world was saying, *If your kids aren't crawling by a certain age, there's an issue, and if they skip crawling and go straight to walking, they must be a genius.* I felt this pressure then, more than 20 years ago, and it is even harder to navigate now. We're flooded with endless highlights of family adventures and who's doing what, where, and when. To me, it always felt like a never-ending stream of curated moments that made other people, including myself, question their own choices and wonder if they were measuring up.

I also found gender stereotypes to be incredibly frustrating. Opinions and judgments seemed to pop up everywhere. "Pink and Barbie dolls are for girls." "Blue and trucks are for boys." "Boys should play rough." "Girls should be quiet and polite." "Sports are for boys, and ballet is for girls." As TV, movies, and books would have it, Cinderella was where it started and stopped—defining relationships and the roles within them as examples for us to follow. On one hand, I could see how you could allow the fantasy to be just that—a fantasy where you get lost in a narrative with no strings attached. But for me, that wasn't the case. I felt deeply that these stories and standards were influencing my children, which like I mentioned before activated the protective part that had me pause, ask "who am I," "what do I believe," ultimately uncovering my truth.

I remember when many of my daughter's friends were playing with Barbie dolls, and I was faced with the decision to buy her one. My stomach flipped, which made me question whether I wanted to introduce her to what can be perceived as a fantasy—a polished image that influenced how girls should dress, look, and even dream about their future. I was activated and knew I had to listen.

At the time, Barbies had a strong presence, and I recognized that familiar Cinderella narrative—the storytelling girls needed completion from outside themselves, that Prince Charming would someday make them whole. I wanted my daughter to craft her own identity, free from thoughts that her Prince Charming would one day come to her rescue. I wanted her to know that she possessed the power to live life successfully herself. That she could speak up, protect herself, and ask for help when she needed it.

Similarly, I wanted my son to understand that it isn't his responsibility to take care of someone else in the way society often expects men to do—that he doesn't need to play the role of Prince Charming, swooping in to save the day. That his worth isn't defined by how much he can provide or take care of his partner, sister, or anyone else. Instead, it's about being whole within himself, happy, feeling complete, and being able to show up authentically.

After navigating all these societal expectations and pressures, you might wonder: How did I know these narratives were not the right path for me? The answers always came through my body. My body spoke with sensations that I couldn't ignore. If I were aligned, I would feel a calm presence, and if I were misaligned, my stomach would flip, my heart would race, and my head would get scorching hot. That is how I knew what was being presented was not right for me and that I needed to get quiet with myself and listen to the guidance that was wanting to be heard.

It can feel intense living in an elevated state because awareness takes hold, and we cannot unsee or unfeel it. **The good news is that inside of awareness lives so much opportunity for growth that can elevate you even more. You just have to be ready to listen, trust what you hear, and allow it to be your guide.**

The cool thing about this level of connection is that it's never too late to re-engage, remember, and allow lessons from the past to inform you now. Here are some scenarios you can reflect on to see if there was a lesson you may have passed over. Has someone recently challenged or irritated you? If so, ask yourself why. It might be because you're envious of what they said or how they said it. Did they show a level of confidence you want to be able to embody, or did what they said trigger something within yourself that needs attention or healing? Maybe someone inspired you recently. If so, you might want to ask yourself why. *Why did this affect me so positively? What can I learn from this?*

Can you think back on a difficult relationship, situation, or health challenge that made you redefine what truly matters to you? What unexpected wisdom revealed itself from that experience? My invitation to you is when you feel an overwhelming emotion, pause, bodyset and reflect on what and why you might be experiencing it. Look at the people in your life and the challenges you face as opportunities for growth. What might these "teachers" be revealing that can expand your awareness even more?

YOUR BODY'S WISDOM IN ACTION

Hopefully by now, you're able to notice your nudges and see them as valuable information guiding you toward what's right. Here's a practical way to create a daily practice that transforms awareness into empowered action.

Notice the Nudge (What you've now learned to recognize)

- The pit in your stomach when about to say "yes" to something wrong for you.
- The warmth in your chest signaling that something feels right.
- The relief when releasing what no longer serves you.

Listen Deeper (Going beyond basic awareness)

- Place your hands on where you feel the sensation strongest.
- Ask specifically: "Is this pulling me forward or holding me back?"
- Notice if the sensation changes when you consider different options.

Take Action (Responding to your body's intelligence)

- For "pulling back" signals: What boundary needs to be set? Create a gesture that embodies protection or creating space.
- For "moving forward" signals: What does this excitement want? Create a gesture that embodies drawing something closer or opening to receive.
- For "pausing" signals: What does this hesitancy need? Create a gesture that embodies a pause, giving yourself time to feel into what is right.

Here are a few scenarios that may help give some guidance on how to apply the notice, listen and action steps. Imagine your boss asks you to lead a new project. You feel that familiar knot in your stomach. Instead of pushing through it, you pause. You get curious. Maybe this nudge is telling you the timing isn't right, and that's okay. You now have the power to explore this feeling before making a decision you might regret. Or maybe a friend invites you to try a new dance class, and you notice that spark of energy in your chest. That buzz might be your body's way of saying, "Yes, this lights me up!" Now, you're empowered to follow that excitement.

Our body has so much to say and so much to teach us. When we honor the signals, we open ourselves to learning something new about ourselves, and sometimes these moments can become the wisdom we carry forward for years.

Years ago, in my 20s, I attended a yoga workshop that felt deeply spiritual. The instructor guided us through a meditation journey that brought me into a deep state of quiet. As I lay on the ground, there were visuals of light pouring into my heart and opening me up in ways I never imagined. I started to cry. The class ended and my body didn't want to move, so I decided to just lie there for a bit. The teacher came over and gently placed her hand on my heart. What started as a soft cry quickly became a hysterical one. Before I knew it, I was cradled in her lap with her arms around me. I remember being so confused and saying, "I don't know why I'm crying," and she said, "You don't have to." That one line made such an impact on my life and became part of my core beliefs.

Too often, we're asked to justify our feelings or told they are not valid because the person we are in conversation with may not understand. Have you experienced people saying things like, "It's not that sad—why are you crying?" Or, "Why are you wearing so many layers? It's not that cold." But here's the thing: If I'm crying, I'm sad.

If I am layered up, I'm cold. What we feel is real, and no one can take that away from us unless we let them.

This is living elevated—embracing our emotions without apology. Knowing that your feelings are valid simply because you feel them. No justification needed. The only permission needed is from you, to be authentically you.

I'm about to share a story that feels incredibly vulnerable. It's the first time I'm writing it out for the world to see. I share it because it reflects the hardest choice I've ever made, a choice I believe many of us can relate to. It's a choice that began as a whisper, grew into a strong nudge, and eventually became a scream that could no longer be ignored. I was being faced with an important choice: the choice to choose me.

COURAGE AT THE CROSSROADS

I met my husband when I was 32, and he was 35. We were perfect partners to navigate young love and parenthood. I loved how our similarities were complementary, and the differences allowed us to grow. Our life was good, and yet, as I entered our second decade, I knew I needed to make a change. I also knew my choice would be misunderstood because, to many people, it looked like I had it all. From an external perspective, everything appeared perfect. We had two amazing kids and a beautiful home. We lived in trendy Brooklyn and had great jobs that we loved. On one hand, they were right; we had so much, and on the other, there was something missing for me. I walked around with an ache, a nudge in my chest that was trying to get my attention. For a while, I just noticed, not doing anything about it yet, but over time, the ache grew into an undeniable call. I remember realizing that the pain I felt came from loving so much of what we had, yet knowing that we were growing apart.

Just because I wanted to leave didn't mean I had stopped loving him. My love had just changed, and I needed something different. To many, that reason wouldn't be enough. "How could you want more when you have so much already?" I've come to learn that what people define as "having so much" varies to a large degree. Some define *so much* by the number of vacations you take or the big house you live in, how many cars you drive and what type they are, what jewelry you wear, or the perks you have at an event. Of course, those things are fun to have, but they represent outward markers of success. What I longed for, I couldn't have. It was deeply personal, and only I could feel its absence.

I had sleepless nights with unlimited tears. Hurting him was going to hurt me too. Countless scenarios played on a loop in my mind, weighing heavily on my heart and stirring up a whirlwind of emotions about how this would impact my children. I had to see myself through the darkness, find the light and grieve what I wished for but couldn't have. I was living with this inner turmoil, desperate for someone to tell me what to do while battling what I knew had to be done.

Societal conditioning dictates so much of how we measure ourselves. How smart you are is determined by a test score and the success of a marriage is determined by how long it lasts. **By leaving, I risked being labeled as someone whose marriage had failed, all the while feeling as though my marriage was one of the greatest successes of my life.** Because I had done the internal work, I was strong enough to stand in my truth and not allow the external world to get in my way. I knew that as long as I proceeded from a place of love and honesty, I could stand proud, brave and strong in my choice. With that said, it was one of the hardest things—if not the hardest thing—I have ever done.

It didn't help that I was constantly reminded of society's view on divorce. Questions would show up about how I would make it on my own. I would also hear statements like, *"You should stay for the kids,"* or *"It's better to settle than to start over."* I heard all of it. Yet, no matter how overwhelming it felt, **I always returned to my body—listening and knowing it was speaking my truth. Those aches were messages and it was up to me to listen.**

The misalignment was growing, and I could literally feel it every-where. An energy would rush through my body and into my head. Many times, it would be a sensation of massive heat and overwhelm. Afterwards, my body would shut down, unavailable and quiet. It would take me a long time to get back to a place of connection. Another thing I noticed was my constant craving for walks. It wasn't just an occasional desire to stretch my legs or clear my head—it became a regular escape, something I did more often than not. These walks were moments I needed to process my emotions and try to make sense of what was happening. Over time, I realized that this repeated urge to step away and find space was my body's way of telling me something may need to change.

Trusting myself required work, especially when faced with con-flicting opinions from the outside world. I looked for guidance from therapists, friends, and family, hoping for clear-cut answers, but ultimately, I realized that the only path to clarity was within me. Despite the loneliness I felt, I recognized its potential for profound transformation and growth. I came to understand that staying true to myself meant seriously considering leaving the marriage, even if it meant walking this path alone.

I was scared—one might say terrified. I feared the future and how I would make everything work. I worried about how my kids would feel, I stressed over the uncertainty ahead, and how I would maintain the lifestyle we had built together. I would go to sleep at night, curled up in my blanket, so sad because I never thought I could be on the brink of hurting the people I loved the most. That was the hardest part. I remember questioning, did my needing change make me a bad person, or did it make me brave? Aren't I just being honest? Can't love change? Why does a successful marriage equate to a forever commitment? Can't it still be successful if it doesn't go for the rest of our lives? I was battling these questions, societal expectations and truths within me for quite some time. Then, I realized something really important: as long as I proceeded from a place of love and honesty, I could stand proud, brave and strong in my choice. That understanding and belief are what gave me the permission to continue on. What mattered most was ensuring that my path was led by my own truth, not shaped by the expectations of others. I reminded myself that those who truly knew and understood me would support my choices, and that was all I needed.

When I finally told him how I felt, I found it hard to communicate what I was feeling, and he found it hard to understand. This was the part that scared me the most. I wanted to be able to explain my feelings in a way that would be understood by the person I had just spent 20 years of my life with and whom I deeply cared for. However, I knew one of the main differences in our marriage was how we processed reasoning, so his confusion didn't surprise me. He leaned heavily on logic, requiring a roadmap with a lot of details. On the other hand, I could find my way through a conversation with few words and more energy and body language. Neither way is wrong or better than the other; it's just a fundamental difference that I struggled with and knew I would have to face when trying to explain my decision to leave. Before that conversation, I made a commitment. I told myself I would allow my body to lead and trust that however I communicated this decision, it would be enough.

What I have come to accept and honor is that our bodies know. They know what we need. They know how we truly feel, what we stand for, what lights us up, and when it's time to let go. The hard part is knowing what to do with that information. **I had to remind myself that fear didn't mean I was on the wrong path; it just meant**

I was scared. Doubt didn't mean that it wasn't the right decision; it was just a part of me trying to protect myself from doing something I may regret. It was hard to make sense of the voices inside to decipher what was real. At the end of the day, I knew—but it took me surrendering, being honest, and finding a way to believe that I would be okay.

A few days after our conversation, he made a comment that I will never forget. He said, "I hope you find what you are looking for." This moment made an imprint that will be with me for the rest of my life. As soon as he made that statement, I heard a whisper say, "I already have; I found me." I remember pausing in awe. I couldn't get over the surge of energy that I felt. It was a presence within telling me that what I was doing was exactly right. I wasn't looking for anything else; I was looking for me.

In that moment, I realized that I came home to my soul, feeling many things at one time—sadness because it was over, frustration because I couldn't explain how I was feeling in a way that he could understand, freedom in my body, and pride for the willingness to step into the hardest moment of my life.

Courage is something we all carry within us, even if it feels buried at times. It's important to remember that it's there and to trust it because, in the end, no one can make our tough choices for us, only we can. Whether you're stepping into a new identity you've hidden out of fear, navigating a major life transition, or having a conversation where you finally ask for what you need, every courageous choice brings you closer to your most aligned and authentic self.

A study by Antonio Damasio on "somatic markers" shows that our bodies provide intuitive signals that guide better decisions by linking emotional experiences with cognitive reasoning. When you honor your truth, you give yourself the permission to evolve in ways you may have never imagined. We realize that what once seemed impossible becomes possible. From my own experience, I have learned that when we trust our body's wisdom, there's no limit to how far we can elevate our life. It can feel hard, AND feel pretty amazing all at the same time.

COMING HOME: THE JOURNEY FORWARD

As we reach the end of our journey together, I want to pause and acknowledge what you've accomplished. The pages you've turned weren't just filled with words—they were invitations to return home to the wisdom that has always lived within you. My hope is that you now recognize that your body has been speaking all along, and now, because you are listening, you've unlocked a profound connection to your inner truth. This is not the end, but a new beginning—a life led with awareness, courage, and alignment.

WHAT I WANT YOU TO KNOW

The path of coming home to ourselves isn't a destination but instead a practice—one that requires courage, patience, and compassion. Throughout these chapters, we've explored stories of transformation that may have resonated with your own experience: the executive who finally addressed the exhaustion that was signaling burnout, the parent who recognized their anxiety when trying to create boundaries, the artist who unlocked creativity when feeling their body respond to music, the partner who feels numb and no longer attracted to the person next to them.

These weren't just stories—they were mirrors reflecting the universal truth that our bodies hold the keys to our truth. What I want you to know, above all else, is that the disconnection you may have felt—from your body, your truth, your power—was not a flaw but a natural response to a world that often asks us to silence our inner knowing. Yet, within that disconnection lies an invitation—a chance to rediscover the wisdom and strength that have always been within you. The framework I've shared—the 3 E's, Embody, Empower, and Elevate—isn't about fixing what's wrong; it's about remembering what's right and trusting its guidance.

WHAT I HOPE MOST FOR YOU

As you close this book, I hope you feel a sense of possibility. To know that the weight of being trapped in patterns, relationships, or circumstances that no longer serve you is not permanent. To know that you have a choice to take action by listening to the wisdom within you. Allowing it to guide you toward what it is you want most in this lifetime. I hope you feel validated by your body's wisdom. Those intuitive hits, those gut feelings, that tension in your shoulders when something isn't aligned with your values—knowing that all of it matters and is a message with meaning. All of it is intelligence. Most importantly, I hope you feel a renewed relationship with your body—not as something to control, perfect, or ignore, but as your most loyal ally in creating a life of fulfillment and purpose.

WHAT I INVITE YOU TO DO

Now comes the part where knowing and feeling transform into action. The framework of the 3 E's gives you the roadmap.

Embody: Begin each day with The Power of Gesture bodyset to anchor yourself in present awareness. Place one hand on your heart, one hand on your belly and close your eyes. Notice your breath and scan your body to connect with the feeling you are experiencing. If there is tension, place your hand on that part of your body and send it love by saying, "I am love", "I am safe", or "I am grateful". Invite your hands to move into gestures that feel supportive. The key is to allow your hands to assist you in celebrating and/or transforming the energy into something that feels aligned. Three to five minutes is enough. Meet yourself where you are at—decide what feels right and follow that guidance without judgment and instead with love.

Empower: When facing decisions throughout your day, pause and check in with your body. Feel what's happening inside before choosing. Is there tightness? Expansion? Warmth? Let these sensations guide you, even when it means saying "no" to something that looks good on paper. Place this reminder somewhere visible: "I commit to listening to my body with patience, trust, and courage." Remember, this isn't about perfection—it's about having the courage to listen and adjust as you go.

Elevate: This is where your personal practice ripples outward. Share what you're learning with others. Show your children what honoring body wisdom looks like. Build your environments—home, work, relationships—around your core values. When you live with this integrity, you create spaces where authenticity becomes natural. You join a community of travelers finding their way home to their inner wisdom, no longer trapped in old stories. One gesture, one breath, one moment of listening at a time.

MAKING THE POWER OF GESTURE A HABIT

The Power of Gesture is meant to be a practice beyond this book—for you to use in your everyday life, as much as you need it. And by the way, you'll want to, because once you experience its transformative effects, you'll recognize how valuable this practice becomes when life inevitably throws you off center.

The truth is, even when something resonates, it can be easily forgotten. Not because it doesn't work, instead because we're human.

Life can pull us in many directions and we forget the importance to pause, bodyset, realign, and remember how strong and capable we are. For whatever reason, self care tends to be the first thing to go, not prioritizing it the way we "should". Now, I don't like to use the word should, however, in this case, I am allowing myself to use it because I believe that our self care is more important than anything.

You'll have several opportunities to experience The Power of Gesture throughout this book. Before you do, I want to share a few ways to make this practice a part of your daily routine:

This practice isn't about perfection. It's about deepening self awareness.

1. Write the word "gesture" on a sticky note and place it on your bathroom mirror, your fridge, or your computer—anywhere you'll see it often.
2. Set an alarm on your phone and name the title of the alarm something like "Check in" or "Gesture time."
3. Add it to your calendar. Schedule it like you would a meeting or appointment.
4. A challenge: For 7 days, make a commitment to start or end your day with one simple gesture. Let your body be the first or the last thing you check in with when you wake up or go to sleep.

This practice isn't about perfection. It's about deepening self awareness. It's about giving yourself small, meaningful moments to return to your truth. That's how this becomes a way of life. One gesture at a time.

ELEVATED SERVICE: LEADERSHIP FROM WITHIN

This is the next evolution of our journey. Here, the inner work trans-forms how we show up as a leader in every area of life—whether guiding our children, supporting our family, leading teams, or chart-ing our own path.

At this level, we are no longer searching outward for validation. We are grounded in self-trust, process emotions skillfully, remain aware of others, and navigate dynamics in ways that serve everyone involved. This is emotional intelligence in action!

I am going to share one final story with you, one that illustrates what it means to truly listen to our body and the incredible trans-formation that unfolds when we do. This story feels like the perfect culmination of everything we've explored together in this book. My hope is that by reading this, you'll feel inspired to pay even closer attention to the nudges within you, knowing it's their guidance that can lead to some of the greatest gifts of your life.

ANSWERING THE CALL

When the 2020 COVID pandemic hit, I was at a place in my life where the work of embodiment and empowerment had taken deep root within me. Self-trust had become the backbone of my existence, allowing subtle nudges, instincts, and voices that, while not obvious to others, were guiding me in my life. At the start of the pandemic, I felt a strong call within me—one that inspired curiosity, eventually leading me to share my gifts and ultimately create a body of work that would elevate both my own life and hundreds of others.

As I mentioned at the beginning of this book, the pandemic birthed The Power of Gesture through necessity and intuition. But what I haven't shared is the deeper journey of how answering this call transformed not just my work, but the lives of hundreds of women who found their voices through this practice.

Despite the unknown and the fear, I began to walk a path that felt more natural than anything I had ever experienced. I surrendered to not knowing where I was headed and chose to trust the guidance from within. I began by reaching out to women I knew and asking if they would place their trust in what I was being led to do. As much as this path was unclear, I knew that during this time I was meant to help people return to their bodies and remind them of their inner strength.

What happened next was beyond anything I could have planned. The practice I had begun to develop—using hand gestures to embody emotions—evolved into something far greater than I initially realized. It became a storytelling modality during a time when stories were essential for healing. **This embodied practice extended beyond the immediate context of COVID, reaching deep into the souls of people, unlocking parts of themselves that needed to be seen and heard.**

As an artist, I immediately recognized the beauty of these hand gestures and felt compelled to create something beyond the sessions. I transformed each two-hour Zoom conversation into a short video story about their life. I added instrumental music and additional video clips that were inspired by our experience together.

Over two years, I produced 150 short-form video documentaries, which I titled *The herStories Collection*. At their core, they are stories of survival—narratives of triumph over sexual assault, domestic violence, divorce, child loss, and the struggle to remain connected to one's identity with perseverance and strength. These stories showcased the power of embodying vulnerability, sharing what unimaginable struggle looks like while representing courage and resilience. These stories gave the women a chance to see themselves in a new light, to recognize their beauty from a different perspective, and to offer comfort to others, assuring them that they are not alone.

What was crafted as pieces of art inspired by real-life experiences became living examples for others, a source of inspiration when we needed it most. I knew that these stories needed to reach a wider audience, and yet, in isolation, there was nowhere to gather. The vision became clear: I had to create an online platform, an art gallery that would bring a global community together for a transformative experience—one that would inspire, heal, and celebrate humanity. And so, **the EmpowerHer virtual gallery** was born. Hundreds of people came through, finding comfort in seeing themselves in others' struggles through this universal language of the body. They realized they, too, had survived. My mission was to shift the mindset of humanity, one story at a time—and together, we did just that.

What began as an intuitive response to unprecedented isolation transformed into a profound awakening—not just for me, but for hundreds of women who found their voices and reclaimed their stories. The Power of Gesture became more than a practice; it became a doorway through which we all discovered what it truly means to embody, empower and elevate.

It's about surrendering to your truth and allowing it to guide you toward what matters most. Through creating the herStories Collection, I witnessed firsthand how choosing authenticity ripples outward, touching lives in ways we could never predict.

Living elevated isn't reserved for extraordinary circumstances—it's available in every moment, through every choice. It's a commitment to living from the inside out, allowing your body's wisdom to lead the way.

- **Living Elevated is** listening to "the call," even when you're not sure where you're going.
- **Living Elevated is** pursuing your passions despite the fear of failure.

- **Living Elevated is** setting boundaries even if it means disappointing others.
- **Living Elevated is** being present to enjoy the simple pleasures and moments in life.
- **Living Elevated is** advocating for what you believe in, even when others are afraid.
- **Living Elevated is** celebrating your individuality, regardless of pressures to conform.
- **Living Elevated is** stepping outside of your comfort zone to pursue personal growth.
- **Living Elevated is** standing up for justice, even when it requires challenging existing power structures.
- **Living Elevated is** standing by yourself even when you "wish" you felt differently.
- **Living Elevated is** choosing authenticity over conformity, even if it means standing alone.
- **Living Elevated is** embracing the grief that comes with making tough decisions.
- **Living Elevated is** listening to your body when it's at odds with your mind.
- **Living Elevated is** choosing your own path, even when your family pressures you to follow theirs.
- **Living Elevated is** expressing your style, beliefs, or sexuality unapologetically, knowing your authenticity is your greatest strength.
- **Living Elevated is** ending a relationship that's no longer right for you, even when it hurts.
- **Living Elevated is** where you no longer resist discomfort but instead welcome it enough to realize that everything is happening *for you*, not *to you*.

LET'S SUMMARIZE WHAT WE KNOW

1. In this elevated state of awareness, we are able to listen to our nudges and turn them into action because we know these physical sensations carry essential messages about our truth.
2. True leadership stems from listening to the body's wisdom, trusting our instincts, and leading with self-awareness and integrity.
3. Your body has been speaking to you all along—and now you know how to listen. When you trust this intelligence and live from this truth, you don't just transform your own life—you become living permission for others to do the same.

Embody. Empower. Elevate.

This is the moment where all the work comes together—where you create a moving mantra designed to **honor** the lessons and feelings of having become embodied, feeling empowered, and living elevated. Being that this is the last time we will experience The Power of Gesture in this book, we are going to do this one a little differently. First, you will be creating three gestures instead of two, which will give you the opportunity to embody each phase. Second, I will give you three suggested gestures to work with so that you can see how simple this is when adding more gestures.

I'm going to modify it here; however, you can experience a longer version by scanning the QR code at the end of this chapter or by visiting www.jenaks.com/yourbodyisspeaking, where you will find The Power of Gesture chapter videos. Press play, and I will be there to guide you through the experience.

STEP 1: INTENTION

Find a comfortable seated position and bodyset. Place one hand on your heart and the other on your belly. Close your eyes and take a few deep breaths. Set a clear intention to honor your truth and live from a place of alignment. You can use the one I offer here, or you can create your own. *"I honor my journey. I trust my truth."*

STEP 2: GESTURE #1: EMBODY.

Bend your elbows and put your hands in a position where they are facing one another, palm to palm, with space in between. It's as if you are holding something in front of you, like a beachball; however, that something is your truth, your values, your life experiences, your deep desires. Now, move your hands slowly toward one another as if your entire inner world is coming together in alignment, where you are deeply connected to your power.

STEP 3: GESTURE #2: EMPOWER.

Now that your palms are together and you are embodied, aligned, and feeling strong, you will slowly turn your palms to face the sky as if you are opening a book. Your chin lifts and your chest opens, calling in this profound sense of aliveness and connection to your strength.

STEP 4: GESTURE #3: ELEVATE.

Once your palms are open, allow them to rise, lifting your hands over your head toward the sky. Your gaze goes further up, and your chest expands even more.

STEP 5: INTEGRATE

Integrate Gestures 1, 2, and 3, anchoring in this ritual for true alignment and sense of empowerment. When you play the music, begin moving your elbows upward and allowing your palms to face inward, then open up to a book and rise to the sky. Repeat the sequence as many times as you desire while calling in your highest self.

It is this self that's within you already. You are simply honoring it and giving it an opportunity to speak..

The gestures you have created in this book are a series of "personalized moving mantras," a vocabulary that you created and can call on at any time. They are the physical expression of your truth, a ritual that has been created to help you remember and connect to the essence of who you are. This practice is something to return to so that you can anchor yourself in the present while inspiring you to rise into the most honest expression of yourself.

TIPS FOR GESTURE PRACTICE

- **Bodyset:** Place one hand on your heart, one hand on your belly, and close your eyes.
- **Move slowly**: Allow yourself to express and listen to what your body is saying.
- **Repeat:** Repetition gives the body more time to process and communicate.
- **Music:** Choose a piece of music that inspires you.

STEP 7: JOURNAL

I invite you to document how your body feels after the practice and reflect on any new realizations that may have been made.

> **Empowered affirmation:** *"I rise with strength, live my truth unapologetically, and soar toward infinite possibilities."*

Ready to dive deeper? This QR code will take you to The Power of Gesture: Embody. Empower. Elevate. video, where you'll join me for a full immersive experience that brings these concepts to life.

I LEAVE YOU WITH THIS

Your Body Is Speaking is not just a concept; it's a call to action. It's an invitation to honor who you are, trust the wisdom within you, and step boldly into a life that is yours to claim now. This call to action is rooted in something familiar but forgotten—a deep innate intelligence that has always been within you—an intelligence that guided our ancestors through every challenge they faced, helping them survive and thrive. That same intelligence is within you.

Your body's signals are the steady and trusted compass that can lead you to clarity, purpose, and fulfillment. Depending on how old you are and the experiences you've lived through, this concept may feel unfamiliar, even foreign. But, it is one worth paying attention to because the consequences of not listening to your body are profound.

When we're not listening, we are disconnected, losing touch with the very intelligence that has kept humanity alive for centuries. By not listening to our bodies, we might find ourselves living in a constant state of overwhelm, uncertainty, or anxiety, driven more by external pressures than our inner truth. When we choose to listen, we feel the freedom of letting go of seeking external validation and returning to the innate confidence to challenge the status quo.

Every social movement that has ever created lasting change began with individuals who dared to listen to that voice within saying, "This isn't right"—a voice that speaks first through the body before the mind can articulate it. **Your body isn't just speaking to you about your personal path. It's speaking to you about the world we could create together.**

So remember, just as our ancestors instinctively trusted their bodies to guide them through the world, you, too, have that capacity within you. It's not lost; it's waiting to be remembered and reignited. One by one, by deepening our self-awareness, understanding our truth, and strengthening our ability to stand by it, we will elevate our collective consciousness, creating a ripple effect that empowers others to do the same and ultimately uplifts humanity.

I invite you to align with the 3 E's framework on a regular basis, remembering that they're not just a framework—they're your road-map to living fully in your truth, and The Power of Gesture helps you get there.

Embody is your awakening, where you reconnect with your inner wisdom and remember the strength that's always been within you. **Empower** turns that awareness into action. Your gestures become anchors of confidence, helping you own your story and make choices that align with your truth. **Elevate** is where fulfillment and service merge, quieting the constant call for external validation and inviting an internal knowing. It's where we are able to let go of distractions and empower our purpose. This phase is where service becomes the natural, outward expression of this inner wholeness. Everything you need to know about who you are and what you truly desire is within you. The world is waiting for you. *Your body is speaking; it's time to listen.*

ACKNOWLEDGMENTS

Each person mentioned here has shaped this book's creation in unique ways they may never fully understand—every interaction has been a lesson, expanding my heart and deepening my understanding of what it means to be truly human.

To my two incredible children, **Alex and Naia**: This book would never have emerged without you. Raising you has challenged the deepest parts of me and forced me to define who I am and want to be in this world. It's because of my love for you that I asked myself what matters most and found those answers within me. You continue to humble and inspire me every single day of my life. I love you.

To my **Mom**: You're the strongest woman I know. Your voice has been a direct line to my soul from the beginning. You've always seen me, encouraging me with an unwavering belief and knowing that the gifts inside my soul weren't just for me—they were for the world. I am forever grateful for your influence and the impact you have made in my life.

To my brothers, **Allan Aks and Stephen Aks**: You are two of my greatest teachers. You have taught me the power of love and how it can create a home so strong inside the body that no time or distance can come between. Your presence in my life guides me daily, and your belief in me has shaped not just this book, but how I show up in the world. I love you both madly!

To **Bob Fink (Dad)**: You entered my life at such a young age with an unshakable belief in me that absolutely shaped how I see myself and how I show up in the world. Your spirit is with me every single day—guiding me, nourishing me, supporting and encouraging me to keep going. I think about you every day.

To **Bob Aks (Dad)**: I thank you for your example as an educator and author. You helped me fill in several educational voids in my life with a loving guidance that I will be grateful for forever. Our relationship has taught me so much and I love you for all of it!

To **Michael**: The lessons I learned and the love we shared allowed me to grow and expand in ways I never imagined possible. I am forever grateful for the family we built, which continues to teach me about love, growth, and resilience every single day.

To **Ellen Weinstein** and **Kay Gaynor**: I write your names and get choked up. Your unwavering belief in my ability as a teaching artist, choreographer, and educator has touched my soul in the most life-shifting way. Your trust in me elevated my existence in all aspects of life. Thank you.

To **National Dance Institute's Students**: For close to two decades, you reminded me every day what excellence looked like. It's when we are seen for who we are that we rise into our greatest potential.

To the **Women in the herStories Collection**: You trusted me during one of the most uncertain times in our history—the 2020 COVID Pandemic. It's your vulnerability and willingness that became the portal for me to create The Power of Gesture, the 3 E's framework, and to do some of the most challenging personal work of my life. You redefined what resilience and survival look like, and you will forever be a gigantic inspiration in my life!

To **Gina Pero & Bernadette Pleasant**: Two of the most outstanding coaches who challenged me to pause and remember who I am. You both taught me how to stand in my story with pride, conviction, and confidence. I am forever grateful.

To **Nancy Levin**: Your generosity, expertise, and heart have opened doors for me and have helped me expand in ways I didn't know I could. You are a gift to so many, and I am truly honored and grateful to have you in my life.

To **Amber Vilhauer**: Your genius goes way beyond books and business. Your ability to see inside someone's soul and know exactly what they need to do next is a rare gift. When I doubted, you believed. When I hesitated, you gently pushed. When I couldn't see the path forward, you illuminated it with a clarity that left me no choice but to go. I adore you!

To **Kate Aks**: You not only inspired the title of this book, you combed through the manuscript with your finest eye, your greatest attention, and your commitment to this message. Wow, do I love and appreciate you!

To **Robin Rinaldi**: Your editing genius is what helped me shape, define, and gain clarity on what this book was meant to be. You have a masterful ability to see the path forward and get to the point quickly, all while holding the energy and essence of the author. I appreciate you so much!

To **Amber Parr Burdett** and **Ashley de Tello**: I am so grateful for your support in editing this book in its last, yet crucial stages. It was your talent and strong intuition that helped me dig deeper within my soul to bring forward the message I didn't realize was still waiting to be expressed. I thank you for challenging me in the most loving way.

To **Rennie Pincus**: I believe in divine timing because of you. When I least expected it, you dropped into my life like an angel, as if you were sent on a mission to see me through this journey. 111, 333, 444, 999—I surrendered and, as a result, received some of the greatest guidance, support, and love in my life.

To **My Ladies:** You know who you are. Your friendship inspires me every single day and always brings me back to what is most important. Your support through the biggest transition of my life impacted my ability to write this book—deep gratitude forever!

A special mention to **Brooke Stewart:** The friend who walked alongside me during the spiritual awakening that led me to this work. You are the one who knew this was a book before it was a book. You saw it before I did. You encouraged and, I would dare to say, "insisted" that I take the wisdom from my body and put it onto paper for the world to see. I am forever grateful to you!

ABOUT THE AUTHOR

Jen Aks is a Leadership Coach, Author, and Speaker who is devoted to empowering individuals to awaken their body's wisdom and tap into their innate intelligence, enabling them to lead with clarity, confidence, and authenticity. Drawing on over 30 years as a dance educator, trainer, and speaker, she brings an understanding of how movement, emotion, and self-awareness intersect to create lasting transformation.

At the core of Jen's work is The Power of Gesture, her signature bodyset practice using hand gestures to process emotion and access inner truth. This innovative approach emerged from her extensive experience in dance education, research in somatics, and two forms of intelligence, emotional and kinesthetic. The Power of Gesture isn't just another mindset technique—it's a revolutionary bodyset practice that creates immediate shifts when traditional approaches fall short. Through this work, Jen has helped thousands of clients break free from limiting patterns, connect with their authentic voice, and embody leadership in a way that allows them to make decisions aligned with their deepest values.

While supporting executives through pivotal decisions, helping teams reconnect and align, or guiding individuals through life's crossroads, Jen's approach leads people back to the most trustworthy guide they have—the wisdom of their own bodies.

Jen believes that mastering your own emotions and understanding those of others is the key to unlocking both personal fulfillment and professional success. Her clients describe her as "the perfect blend of nurturing and challenging," creating safe spaces where powerful shifts occur through a simple yet profound practice that honors the intelligence that has always resided within us.

www.ingramcontent.com/pod-product-compliance
Lightning Source LLC
Chambersburg PA
CBHW031526120626
46545CB00005B/2029